Charter Oak Terrace

Life, Death, and Rebirth of a Public Housing Project

David Radcliffe

Southside Media
Hartford, Connecticut

Library of Congress Catalog Card Number: 98-092892

International Standard Book Number 0-9664182-0-4

Cover Design by Elizabeth Noli

Cover photos by David Radcliffe (cornerstone)
and
Tony DeBonee

Manufactured in the
United States of America
1998

Table of Contents

Introduction

In 1942 Marilyn Romano was thirteen years old when she and her family moved to Charter Oak Terrace, a new 1,000 unit public housing project in the southwest corner of Hartford, Connecticut. She has only fond memories of her time there. "When the doors to the community center opened, kids would line up to get in," recalled Romano years later. "Charter Oak was a family."

In the 1950's and '60's Laura Taylor and her family lived in Charter Oak. She looked up to the many bankers, lawyers, doctors and teachers who had their start in the Terrace. "We had so many role models. Not just athletes, but people who came from the community and became real successes." Her years in the tight-knit community were filled with fun and endless activity. "There was a bus that came around and sold penny candy. We had Pops the ice cream man, Paul the bread man, and Al the fish man. We never had to leave."

Charter Oak was a place where morning glories climbed trellises, children and parents played softball in the courtyard, and neighbors gathered for afternoon tea. It was a place that bubbled with pride and community. It was a starting point, a place of hope. [Reference 146 at end of book.]

As time passed the fortunes of Charter Oak changed. Fifty-two years after the opening of Charter Oak Terrace, in the spring of 1993, a young man named Pablo Rosado drove a red Firebird into the neighborhood. In the passenger seat was Ralph Moreno, who cradled a semi-automatic Tec-9, a vicious assault weapon.

The two were ordered to Charter Oak where a gang called Los Solidos ran a sophisticated and violent drug operation on one side of the now crumbling community. A competing gang known as the Latin Kings controlled the other side. A Solido member was reported to be in trouble.

The young men spotted a car they thought was full of Latin Kings. Rosado pulled the Firebird alongside, and Moreno opened fire. But they had the wrong car. As a result, seven-year-old Marcelina Delgado, who was sitting in the front seat on her mother's lap, was killed. [195]

As gang, drug, and violent activity grew in Hartford, Charter Oak fell apart. In 1995, much of Charter Oak, reported a local newspaper, looked like an abandoned village during a war. Fleeing residents left behind piles of garbage: mops, sneakers, bike tires, broken bottles, washing machines, garbage cans, and mattresses.

At 1 p.m. on Monday, April 22, 1996, the jagged steel jaws of a John Deere excavator closed around the corner of a building on Charter Oak's Victory Street. [196] The razing of Charter Oak had begun.

Today, but for the memories, the Charter Oak that Marilyn Romano knew as a girl in 1942 — and home to more than 50,000 men, women and children for over a half century — is gone. [197]

The following collection of articles, interviews, and other materials tells the story of the life, death, and rebirth of Charter Oak Terrace.

Chapter One

The Birth of Public Housing
1934 to 1940

In the 12 years that Franklin Delano Roosevelt was President, his 'New Deal' effort to help end the Depression and increase employment led to the creation of at least 35 new federal agencies. Government welfare programs began in America, as well as Social Security. This era was one of dramatic increases in the Federal government's role in the health and well-being of the national economy. [238]

One New Deal creation sprang from the United States Public Housing Act of 1937. Through this act, public housing was started by the Federal government to create jobs and to build homes for people who had some money but could not afford private accommodations. [107] There was little choice but to have either cities or states run public housing. In 1935, a Supreme Court ruling prevented the Federal government from clearing land and building projects. So instead of owning and operating public housing, the Federal government gave money to local housing authorities who could be more responsive to local needs. [240]

With its new public housing initiative, the Federal government paid the interest and principal on the mortgages, which where sold to investors by city government agencies to finance the construction of housing for the low income families who would live there. The kind of housing local contractors could build, rules for selecting tenants, and the formulas for setting rents were determined primarily by the Federal government. Rents were based on the occupant family's income. If their income increased, so did the rent. If an income rose above a certain maximum, the family had to move out. [238]

The Hartford Housing Crisis

Hartford, Connecticut in the 1930's desperately needed housing. With a population of 165,000 (up from 138,000 in 1920) packed into 18 square miles, Hartford, the state capital and home to some of the nation's largest insurance companies, had thousands of decrepit housing units and a demand for new units far beyond the supply.

City leaders made early plans to address housing needs. Speaking at a meeting sponsored by the Property Owners, Taxpayers and Citizen's League on December 19, 1934, Herbert Gibson, director of the 'Slum Clearance Survey' and consultant to the mayor's housing committee, described in detail the two federal housing projects proposed for Hartford. These developments, said Gibson, were to provide modern housing for "900 white and 640 negro families." [1] Despite this early planning, the first new unit would not be built in Hartford for another six years.

In 1938, Hartford Mayor Thomas J. Spellacy, who served as mayor from 1935 to 1943, announced his appointment of a five-man Housing Authority, the Second in Connecticut, after the city of Bridgeport, to be chaired by Stillman F. Westbrook, vice-president of the Aetna Life Insurance Company. The unpaid appointments became effective on June 1, 1938.

The four others named to the first Housing Authority:

William A. Scott, president of the Hartford Central Labor Union, composed of delegates of most labor unions in this city;

G. Burgess Fisher, president of the George B. Fisher company;

Rev. William K. Hopes, pastor of the Bethel African Methodist Episcopal Church; and,

Bruce Caldwell, attorney and one of the Mayor's law partners. (In his early life, Caldwell played professional baseball with the Cleveland Indians and football with the New York Giants.)

Hartford Housing Authority Board of Commissioners, 1942. (Left to right) Mrs. Lee, Bruce Caldwell, William A. Scott, Berkeley Cox, Rev. William K. Hopes, M. Allyn Wadhams, and Russel H. Allen.

The Authority became a public corporation set up by an Act of the Connecticut Legislature and established by the City Council and the Mayor in the appointment of the Commissioners of the Authority. While the Authority is administratively independent of the municipal government, the city council has taken the position that functionally the Housing Authority is a part of the local government and aims to work as a companion agency. [48]

The new Hartford Housing Authority was located at 650 Main Street until early 1940, when it moved to 525 Main Street.

Russel H. Allen became the Authority's first executive secretary (the position was later executive director) on September 1, 1938. Allen was hired for $6,000. His position was similar to that of the president of a corporation, with members of the Authority acting as a board of directors with power to approve and disapprove his acts.

Allen was 53 years old and married. He graduated from DePaul University in 1906 with a bachelor of philosophy degree. He was an instructor in German, Latin and history at Baker University, among other places. He also studied in Europe. From 1914 to 1920, Allen served on the staff of the Bureau of Municipal Research in New York City, where he conducted surveys and wrote reports on urban issues.

While at the Bureau Allen was Executive Secretary to Charles A. Beard, a noted historian and director of the Bureau of Municipal Research. The Bureau was the spearhead of municipal reform not only in New York City but throughout the United States. A memorable confrontation between Beard and another young researcher at the Bureau, Robert Moses, is recorded in Robert Caro's book the "The Power Broker." What impact might these powerful experiences of urban development have had on Russel H. Allen and the ideas he would bring with him to Hartford? [17, 239]

The Hartford Housing Authority Gets to Work

The first job for the fledgling Authority was to determine the city's "slum area and to prepare plans for a slum clearance and subsidized housing project". Toward that end, the Authority was to apply to the United States Housing Authority for Federal funds to be earmarked to Hartford. (The United States Housing Authority was renamed the Federal Public Housing Administration in 1942, then the Public Housing Administration in 1947. It became the Department of Housing and Urban Development (HUD) in 1965. [2])

Time was of the essence. In April 1940, before the formal involvement of the United States in World War II, Hartford had a housing vacancy rate of just 1.2% percent. Many poor and working class families could not find decent housing.

The population of Hartford was 95 percent white, but blacks, although numbering just 2,000 families in Hartford at the time, were particularly hard-hit by the severe housing crisis that faced the city. A 1941 survey of the Hartford housing situation by a Works Project Administration (WPA) field force showed that 80 percent of the city's black population was concentrated in a 40 square block area in northern Hartford. This area was bounded on the south by Homestead Avenue, on the west by Garden Street, on the north by Westland Street, and on the east by Windsor Street. [229]

Conditions there were dreadful. In early 1942, Dr. Allen F. Jackson, president of the local branch of the National Association for the Advancement of Colored

People, said that tuberculosis and disease, attributed to the overcrowding in north Hartford, were increasing steadily.

By 1943, this bad situation grew worse. During that time some 2,000 additional black families moved to Hartford because of the area's defense industry boom. Also, an existing 200 family black-only housing complex on the east side of Hartford's Bellevue Street was in need of demolition.

For the new and dislocated families, there was practically no place to live, said then Welfare Superintendent William J. Ryan. "I don't know what we're going to do with them." [230]

The Hartford Housing Authority came up with a plan to rid the city of its worst housing and build new homes. "Slum elimination can be accomplished in two ways," stated the Authority's 1939 annual report:

> "The Authority can purchase large slum blocks (or acquire them by eminent domain), tear down the existing dilapidated structures and replace them by new construction of its own. Or it can elect to build on vacant land and in the meantime can cooperate with the city in the use of the latter's police powers to encourage the repair, vacation, and demolition of buildings revealed to be in violation of building, health or fire codes." [45]

The Authority noted, in its early planning, that adding 1,700 units of public housing coud have far reaching effects on the economic and social life of the city.

> "In fact, even small additions to house people or business have a definite effect on the character and property values of neighborhoods. The building of an apartment house or store will cause dislocations in populations, changes in property values, and create traffic and parking problems with which the city must contend. Demolition, rehabilitation and conversion of properties from one use to another all definitely affect the pattern of city growth and indirectly in the living conditions of our population." [15]

The Hartford Housing Authority embarked on the city's most ambitious development since the 1890's. In June 1940, ground was broken for Connecticut's first public housing project: a 146 unit, north Hartford complex called Nelton Court. In February 1941, the 222 unit Dutch Point Colony was opened. And on September 28, 1941, the Bellevue Square housing project cornerstone was laid.

At the Bellevue Square ceremony, State Senator Alfred N. Bingham said:

> "Here will be 500 families more with a stake in the democratic way of life, a stake that they lack so long as their country allows their children to grow up in unhealthy back alleys. We can no longer afford slums. We can no longer afford poverty in America. The contest between totalitarianism and democracy is a contest between two ways of life. It must be won on the home front as well as on foreign battlefields." [19]

When these three housing projects were dedicated, the United States was not yet officially involved in World War II. But Hartford and many other American cities saw the storm coming, and were rapidly preparing for the day when the country would soon join the immense global battle.

Chapter Two

Hartford Prepares for War
1940-1941

As the United States drew closer to war, it became even more difficult to find a place to live in Hartford. Thousands of new families were moving to the area, lured by jobs in the growing defense industry.

In 1940 Russel H. Allen, still Director of the Hartford Housing Authority, interviewed the personnel managers of the area's largest defense companies: Colt's Patent Fire Arms Manufacturing Company, Niles-Bement- Pond Company (a division of Pratt and Whitney), and Pratt and Whitney United Aircraft. His purpose was to obtain first-hand information on the current employment situation in their plants and its relation to housing needs in Hartford. Allen recorded the following information:

> Colt's: Mr. Herbert Walker, Personnel Officer
> Personnel during normal employment: 1,845
> Personnel employed at present: 3,082
> Expected increase in force: 400 to 500 by January 1, 1941, 1,000 by August 1, 1941
>
> Extension of plant is underway. Some departments now on three shifts. Departments on two shifts will be put on three shifts as needed.
>
> Pratt & Whitney Division, Niles-Bement-Pond:
> Mr. Frank W. Cooke
> Personnel during normal employment: 2,500
> Personnel employed at present: 3,000
> Expected increase in force: 500 employers in next 6 months, and 500 more in following six months.

Present addition of 500 have come from Hartford area. Some employees from Vermont. Some commuting from Springfield and Holyoke. Need for rents at $35 to $45.

Pratt & Whitney (United Aircraft): Mr. W. F. Burke
Personnel during normal employment: 3,000
Personnel employed at present: 11,000
Expected increase in force: 3,500 to 4,000 employees in next 6 months

With this evidence, Allen summarized the need as "a source of worry for [factories] during the coming period. Present turnover of personnel (1 percent a month) is largely due to lack of local housing. Higher wage rates here [in Hartford] than in Boston, yet workers can not remain in Hartford due to lack of housing." [8]

By September 1941, two months before the attack on Pearl Harbor, there were 52 defense-related industries in the immediate Hartford area. [9] The industry as a whole was expected to add 11,000 workers by the middle of 1942. The demand for housing was clear. But how and where could housing on the scale needed be built in such a short period of time?

War Housing

"The dark, dank hovels, the modern slums of the old city are giving ground in America."

— Robert R. Lewis, 1941 [14]
Real Estate Editor, *Hartford Times*

The first war-related housing project in Hartford was built by Colonel Sam Colt for workers in Colt's Armory during the Civil War. In 1861, his factory was working 24 hours a day. Nearby in South Meadows, Colt built 30 wooden houses to house watch-workers imported by the gun maker from Switzerland to work in the arms plant. Many of these buildings are still occupied today. [14]

Eighty years later, there was very little vacant land left in Hartford on which to build housing in the numbers required by local families. The only available spot was in Hartford's south west corner, 137 acres of mostly open farmland straddling the South Branch of the Park River. The land, surveys reported, "is rolling, with a low point of the plain at about 40 feet in elevation." Through the eastern edge of this land ran Cemetery Brook, a small stream which meandered into the Park River north of Flatbush Avenue. (Flatbush Avenue, circa 1861, formerly known both as Allen's Road and also Commons Road, is said to have been derived from Flatbush Avenue in Brooklyn, New York. Flatbush there and here in Hartford both led to horse racing tracks.) Except for Flatbush Avenue, located along the northern edge of the land, there were no other streets on the parcel. [8]

This land had always been lightly used because of the low elevation and potential for flooding. In 1855, along Cemetery Brook, there were just two businesses: a Sash and Blind Company and the Seymour Brickyard. By the end of the 19th century these two companies were gone, leaving behind only several wood frame buildings surrounded by what is believed to have been farmland.

By 1920, there remained very little development at this site. An atlas shows that much of the land west of the South Branch of the Park River was owned by the Hartford psychiatric hospital that would later be called the 'Institute of Living'. Later, in 1940, three frame, owner-occupied dwellings in fair condition, several sheds and one small dairy building occupied the site of what would become one of the largest public housing projects in New England. The structures were assessed at $7,100.

Transportation for the possible new residents also had to be considered. The land by no means was centrally located. If housing was built, a person would have to walk, or ride a bus or trolley, to downtown Hartford, 2.5 miles to the northeast. The ride took fifteen minutes and cost eight cents in 1941. There were trolleys on New Park Avenue (.4 miles away), New Britain Avenue (.6 miles) and Zion Street (.8 miles). The principal areas of industrial employment were from .25 to 1.75 miles away. [8]

Planning Begins

Although the site may not have been the most accessible or the best to build on — the Park River flooded three times in the 1930's, swamping more than a third of the area — it was the only available parcel of the size needed.

Planning for the defense housing project began in earnest in May 1940. On July 22, an application for financial assistance was submitted to the federal government, and on August 28 President Franklin D. Roosevelt approved the project. By late 1940, the land described above was purchased and the handful of remaining buildings were removed by the General House Wrecking Company of Hartford.

The new chairperson of the Hartford Housing Authority, Berkeley Cox, wrote about some of the early development challenges in an October 1941 newspaper article:

> "Construction of the project has not been all clear sailing. Many people thought last year that a thousand families, government financed project was too big, and it took a conference in Washington between representatives and several government agencies and of the Hartford Authority to decide whether it should be a thousand or five hundred."

Around the country, 200,000 public housing units were being built at 128 different locations to support the need for defense worker housing in advance of World War II. Hartford's ultimate 1,000 units made it the largest defense housing project in New England.

On February 24, 1941, ground was broken on the city's fourth housing project. It would be called Charter Oak Terrace. [46]

There is no evidence to suggest how, when or by whom the name Charter Oak Terrace was given to the project. Federal Works Administrator John M. Carmody wrote in an October 1941 *Hartford Courant* story:

> "Its very name, Charter Oak Terrace, associated as it is with the colonial struggles for liberty seems to me to be of significance, especially in these times. Those citizens who

View of Charter Oak Terrace housing project site, 1940. Flatbush Avenue runs along the bottom of the photo.

> will soon make it their home may well ponder the historic name of Charter Oak."

However, the Charter Oak was an important tree in early Connecticut history. A brief story of the tree, from the State of Connecticut's 'Sites, Seals, Symbols' booklet:

> "On October 9, 1662, the General Court of Connecticut formally received the Charter won from King Charles II of England by Governor John Winthrop, Jr, who had crossed the ocean for that purpose.
>
> "Twenty-five years later, with the succession of James II to the throne, Connecticut's troubles began in earnest. Sir Edmund Andros, His Majesty's agent, followed up failure of various strategies by arriving in Hartford with an armed force to seize the Charter and take back control of Connecticut.
>
> "After hours of debate, with the Charter on the table between the opposing parties, the candle-lit room went suddenly dark. Moments later when the candles were re-lighted, the Charter was gone. Captain Joseph Wadsworth is credited with having removed and secreted the Charter in the majestic oak on the Wyllys estate near downtown Hartford." [241]

The historical significance of the Charter Oak tree made it a popular place name. In the 1941 Hartford telephone directory there were 22 listings that included Charter Oak.

On the dedication of the Charter Oak Terrace housing project, a fragment from the original Charter Oak tree was placed in a time capsule buried in the administration building on Overlook Terrace. "It reposes in a copper box in the cornerstone of the 1,000 family defense housing project," read a news account, "named after the historical tree". [101]

Chapter Three

Charter Oak Terrace
1941

No nation is worthy of fighting for democracy if it is willing to tolerate slums at home.

— Charles F. Palmer, October 4, 1941
U.S. Defense Housing Coordinator

Construction continued on Charter Oak Terrace throughout the spring and summer of 1941. The general contractor was the Cauldwell-Wingate Company of New York City. Fifteen of the 41 different firms that built Charter Oak Terrace were from Hartford. [6]

Charles E. Hungerford, the Technical Director of the Authority, described the physical layout of Charter Oak in a rather complicated 1941 newspaper article:

> "Charter Oak was built on raw unimproved farmland cut into by the South Branch of the Park River. East of the river is called Area A, west of the river Area B.
>
> "The site being heavily wooded in sections and of rolling contours, every effort was made to save existing trees and to layout roads and service drives so as to flow with the contours thus reducing the cost of rough grading to a minimum.
>
> "Service drives were then laid out so as to divide the structures into groups of two rows on each side of the service drives, thus allowing the service side of the dwelling units in all structures to face the service drives and the front or living side of the dwelling units to face each other with a common park area or mall between, all of which were interconnected by main and connecting walks.

> "The rear yard can be utilized as a play area by the small preschool children under the watchful eye of their mother who undoubtedly spends more of her time in the kitchen than in any other room and in all cases, the kitchen faces the rear or service yard." [15]

There were delays in getting materials, which held back contractors somewhat. It is also believed that many of the materials used were not of the highest quality, as the war made the better supplies harder to find and afford.

Years later, Authority Chairman Berkeley Cox's son, Berkeley Jr., who was only 11 when Charter Oak was opened, recalled his father's mixed feelings about it. "He was very disappointed in it because they couldn't get the materials they needed during the war," Cox said. "He also hoped it would look more like a real suburban neighborhood than a housing project." [225]

Despite these challenges, Charter Oak Terrace took just 8 months to build. At the height of construction in August 1941, 1,400 men were working to ready the project for occupancy. [73] Including land, buildings, water, sewer and utilities the entire development cost about $4.5 million.

The Dedication

The *Hartford Courant* ran a three page story on the day of the dedication of Charter Oak Terrace. In one of the October 4, 1941 articles, Federal Works Administrator John M. Carmody wrote about the importance of housing in support of the war effort:

> "To crush the aggressors, the democracies must have the implements of war, and in great quantities. To get these planes, and guns, and tanks in quality and quantity, the workers who make them must have decent homes in which to live."

Charter Oak Terrace was officially dedicated at a widely-publicized ceremony at 3:00 p.m. on Saturday, October 4, 1941.

The ceremony took place on the front steps of the uncompleted administration building on what is now

Construction of Charter Oak, ABC side, 1941.

Overlook Terrace. (The Overlook Terrace name was suggested by the Authority's director Russel H. Allen due to its location along the terrace overlooking the Park River.) [75] Numerous dignitaries spoke with great enthusiasm on the hope for Charter Oak.

"Faced as we are with the greatest danger the country has ever confronted, we must put first things first; and adequate housing for the nation's defense workers is one of these firsts," stated Charles F. Palmer, United States Defense Housing Coordinator.

"Hartford, the Insurance City. That name has been justly famous for generations," Palmer continued. "Now you have become the Defense City."

Hartford's Mayor Thomas J. Spellacy, in a brief address, expressed his pleasure in seeing the project well on its way to completion and his thanks to the United States Housing Authority for its help "without which Hartford might not have been able to accomplish all that it has along that line".

Other remarks at the ceremony were given by Summer K. Wiley, representative of United States Housing Authority, and Rev. E. Dent Lackey, official

Sampling of Charter Oak contractor ads from the October 7, 1941 Hartford Courant

BERKELEY COX
CHAIRMAN
WILLIAM A. SCOTT
VICE CHAIRMAN
BRUCE CALDWELL
TREASURER
REV. WILLIAM K. HOPES
M. ALLYN WADHAMS

HOUSING AUTHORITY
OF THE
CITY OF HARTFORD
ROOM 216 - 525 MAIN STREET

RUSSEL H. ALLEN
EXECUTIVE SECRETARY

HARTFORD, CONN.

October 4, 1941

As commissioners of the Housing Authority, it is our sincere hope that Charter Oak Terrace will substantially benefit all citizens of Hartford and the nation as a whole in its defense effort.

Berkeley Cox
BERKELEY COX

William A. Scott
WILLIAM A. SCOTT

Bruce Caldwell
BRUCE CALDWELL

Rev. William K. Hopes
REV. WILLIAM K. HOPES

M. Allyn Wadhams
M. ALLYN WADHAMS

Note found in Charter Oak cornerstone from Hartford Housing Authority Board of Commissioners.

representative of Governor Robert A. Hurley (1941 to 1943). The program was presided over by Berkeley Cox, Chairperson of the Authority. Rev. George Roberts, president of the Hartford Federation of Churches, gave the invocation, and Rev. John A.

Dooley, pastor of nearby St. Lawrence O'Toole Church, pronounced the benediction. Rabbi Abraham J. Feldman also spoke.

Charles Palmer and Mayor Spellacy wielded the trowels in the cornerstone laying ceremony, which started at 3:30 p.m. on that day.

Before the cornerstone was sealed into its permanent place in the administration building, seventeen items of interest pertaining to the project were inserted in a copper box and placed inside the stone. The contents of the time capsule included:

• A note typed on a sample form of a check and voucher used to pay bills for the Charter Oak Terrace obligations. It read: October 4, 1941. "On this day, the Dedication of the Corner Stone Laying at Charter Oak Terrace, we take the opportunity to extend to the future tenants of Charter Oak Terrace, our sincere best wishes for much HAPPINESS, PROSPERITY and GOOD HEALTH which they may enjoy at this Community."[3]

• Copies of the day's two local newspapers, *The Hartford Courant* (cost: four cents) and *The Hartford Times. The Courant's* front page headlines focused on the war, which the U.S. would not formally enter for another two months. One story line told that a U.S. ship with a crew of 37 was sunk by an enemy torpedo off the coast of Brazil. Another lead story covered a speech given by Hitler, reporting on Germany's progress on the Russian front. Also on the front page was a column on the dedication of Charter Oak Terrace. Inside was a three page spread on the new defense housing.

• A fragment of the original Charter Oak tree, famed in local tradition, was placed in the box by Paul B. Godard, president of the Hartford Real Estate Board. It formerly was in his father's collection of historical relics.

(This time capsule was rediscovered by David Radcliffe of Hartford and opened at a public ceremony in October 1997. Today, the items found in the box are on display in the Hartford Collection of the Hartford Public Library. [10])

Following the ceremony, the gathered crowd walked over to inspect the well-decorated and furnished demonstration unit, located in a court near the intersection of Newfield and Flatbush avenues. At the time, neither grass nor trees had been planted. [73]

The New Charter Oak

When finished, Charter Oak had 40 miles of piping, 17 miles of walks and roads, 15 miles of sewer lines and 12 miles of electrical wiring. [13]

The 137 acre Charter Oak Terrace consisted of 1,000 units housed in 236 buildings made of brick, cinder-block and wood frame in nine different sizes and styles. All had flat roofs. The flooring was of hardwood and asphalt tile. Living rooms and kitchens were on the first floor, bedrooms and baths on the second. A brochure from the day said that the Charter Oak units featured "large airy rooms, painted in pastel shades for a bright and cheerful atmosphere".

The new Charter Oak also had a community center with an auditorium, health clinic and meeting rooms and an administration building for the Authority management staff. Indoor and outdoor play areas were provided. A pamphlet said a shopping center was planned to service the 3,500 people expected to live there.[5]

Given the historic level of activity in and around Hartford at the time, one can imagine the tremendous amount of energy that must have swirled around residents of the day. War was on the horizon. Slums were being rapidly destroyed and new housing was being constructed just as quickly. There were high hopes for the new Charter Oak, which the 1941 first annual report of the Hartford Housing Authority boasted was built to last 60 years or more. [45]

Charter Oak Terrace ABC side, early 1940's.

Charter Oak Terrace, ABC side, 1942. Note newly-planted trees and grass.

Chapter Four

First Families of Charter Oak Terrace 1942

> "Charter Oak stands as a monument to modern construction and planning in the large-scale housing field and as a symbol of the times. When peace is restored, Charter Oak will be no ghost town. The whole project will be re-populated with low income families drawn from the sub-standard houses in Hartford — families who are now compelled to endure their inadequate shelter until the emergency is over." [13]
>
> *Hartford Courant*, October 1941

To be eligible for defense housing, heads of tenant families had to be United States citizens employed in an industry in the Hartford area accredited as a 'defense industry', and be in need of adequate housing. Interested families applied to the Authority office at 650 Main Street, Room 232. [5]

There were 1,700 applications for the 1,000 available units. One applicant for Charter Oak had lived in a tobacco shed, another in a dairy house, and still others in tents and trailer camps. Forty-four percent of the first Charter Oak families came from overcrowded or physically substandard housing. And many applying to Charter Oak were losing valuable time from their jobs looking for an apartment or home. [18] (Thirty percent of the first 1,000 Charter Oak families worked at Colt's, 20.6 percent at United Aircraft Corporation, and 18.6 percent at the Pratt & Whitney Division of the Niles-Bement-Pond.) [16]

Charter Oak young people take in Saturday afternoon movies at the Community Building on Overlook Terrace. June 17, 1944

The first family to move into Charter Oak in late October 1941 was John J. Vail, his wife and their nine children. They had been evicted from a Main Street apartment for reasons unknown today.

In 1942, Charter Oak monthly rents ranged from $34 to $41 based on family income and apartment size up to 5 bedrooms. These rents included water, electricity for lighting and refrigeration, and gas for cooking and water heating. Rents for the 200 two and one-half room units also included steam heat and hot water. The remaining 800 units were heated by tenants themselves by individual hot water heating systems operating from coal fired boilers in utility rooms. These tenants had to buy their own coal. [5]

The homes met the need for Richard Petrus' family. His father worked at Colt Firearms. "They used to have buses come into Charter Oak to bring people to Colt's and other defense plants," Petrus said. His father worked 50 to 60 hours a week, like most of the workers there, and saved money so the family could eventually move out of Charter Oak and buy a house. They lived there two years. [146]

Marilyn (Coughlin) Romano, former Charter Oak resident

My father had died when I was 12. My mother and grandmother worked at a small tool company on New Park Avenue in the defense industry. That's how they got into Charter Oak. We were on Lisbon Street before that.

When we moved in the spring of 1942, work was still being done to finish Charter Oak. Many sidewalks weren't in place yet! We lived at C-79[1], on the left of what is now Cotswold Street[2], near Shorty's grocery.

We jumped rope, and the boys would play football in the grass across from the community center.

We went to church at St. John's. Fr. Skelley was there, and we sang in the choir. Our church was our second home.

I had two brothers, one of whom was called the Mayor of Charter Oak. He knew everyone. He would sing at minstrels we had there. We had Masses, Thursday night dances. When the doors opened kids would line up to get in. There was a small library there too. The community center meant everything to us. Movies were shown there too.

We took buses everywhere. We had to walk to New Park Avenue and take a bus to Park Street to grocery shop, take a bus back and walk with the groceries, stopping every few minutes to put down the bags.

I moved out in the late 1940's when I got married.

Charter Oak was a family. We've had three reunions recently. People had to be turned away because we had too many people come! Everyone wanted to be together. John Wardlaw (Authority director starting in 1977) once heard about one of our reunions. He couldn't believe it. He wanted to meet with me. When we met, he asked why we were having a reunion for Charter Oak Terrace. He was thrilled to help, but just couldn't believe that at one point in time people were so happy to live there.

I still go by Charter Oak now and again. It was my childhood place. A lot of memories come to me when I see it, even today. We still have many life-long friends from Charter Oak. It was a beautiful time of our life.

1. In 1959, Charter Oak was renumbered, along with street names, to conform to other neighborhoods. [91]

2. Cotswold Street in Charter Oak was the idea of Russel H. Allen in 1941. It was made of two old English words, "cotts" meaning cottage, and "wold" meaning grove. Ironically, most of the trees along this street were cut down to make way for more housing.

Charter Oak Families Join War Effort

In 1942, families were flocking to the area for defense jobs and desperately seeking shelter. By this time, the United States was deeply involved in the war.

Because of the concentration of the defense industry, Hartford was one of the most important war-related cities on the east coast. To guard vital city industries from surprise enemy air attacks from the Atlantic, 1,300 soldiers were stationed in Hartford by the end of 1941. [23]

As the local defense industry hummed along, Hartford residents were also involved in the war effort,

Fr. Bill McCarthy, former Charter Oak resident

I lived at A-2, Charter Oak Terrace. We were one of the first tenants in Charter Oak when we moved there in 1941. I was 7 when we moved from Kibbe Street.

We moved because the houses were much nicer in Charter Oak. My dad worked at Arrow-Hart during the war.

There was always something to do. You could always go to Mr. O'Neil [Manager of Charter Oak, who lived at A-1], and he'd come out and give you a baseball. And there was a 'Boy's Brigade' with 900 boys. It was quite a thing. You had stripes — private, corporal and so on. We did marches. It was good discipline. We learned quite a few skills, like the Boy Scouts. Sadie Loranger ran the playground down at the community center. She knew every kid in the Terrace.

Bill Hylton was the famous newspaper man who had an old car. The back of it was all carved out, and filled with *The Courant* and *Times*. He'd come in and count them out. I remembered he had a super-sharp pencil that he use to mark the customers. I was one of the paperboys. To this day I remember the names of everyone I delivered to. The Walsh's. The Lynch's. The Clark's [Owen Clark was a State Representative in the 1940s], Florence's, O'Rourke's, the Cronin's [Joseph Cronin was Mayor of Hartford in the 1950s].

Families were very religious at the time, especially during the War. Whenever there was a social function, there would be prayers and singing of 'God Bless America', which Kate Smith had just come out with at the time. People were unified, and there was a great deal of energy. There was perceived a common enemy, and that really brought people together.

changing daily life in almost every way. Common materials were in short supply, leading to rationing and recycling.

Eleanor B. Kennelly was appointed by Mayor Spellacy to chair the Hartford War Price and Rationing Board. She coordinated issuance of ration books. [26] One day, a man who applied to the Board for more oil to heat his room was asked by the clerk: "Have you any other means of heating this room? "Lady" he replied, "the only thing I have is an electric light bulb."

(Kennelly taught for ten years at the Washington Street school in Hartford from 1920 to 1930. She was active at St. Lawrence O'Toole Church and lived at 62 Cumberland Street. The Eleanor B. Kennelly School in southwest Hartford was named in her honor. One of her children was James, who later in life became the Speaker of the House for Connecticut. James Kennelly married Barbara Bailey, who became a city councilperson, U.S. Congressperson, and in 1998, candidate for Governor of Connecticut.)

Salvage bins were placed in city school yards for metal, rubber and rags. Mayor Thomas J. Spellacy made a direct appeal to children to help — ". . . bring rubber to the nearest filling station!" he cried in an open letter. Residents were encouraged to save kitchen fats valuable in the production of explosives: "Housewives recruited to save fats in struggle against Axis" read a headline. One would receive four cents a pound for all household grease saved. [20]

An article from the time told how to respond in the event of an air raid. Among the 15 things to do were: "If a gas bomb falls, spray with water."; "Keep calm"; and, "Stay at home". Sand was available at 36 spots in Hartford, useful for extinguishing incendiary bombs. Nearest to Charter Oak, sand could be had at the southeast corner of Flatbush Avenue opposite Community Place (later the office of the Hartford Housing Authority). [24]

In February 1942, 21,000 Hartford men between 20 and 44 years old registered for the draft. Charter Oak residents registered at the Wilson Street School or Fire Station 15 on New Britain Avenue. [25]

Dan Lynch, former Charter Oak resident

We moved to Charter Oak, C-58, from Merrill Street in 1943. I was 10. We moved out by 1950. My father worked for Pratt and Whitney, my mother at the Royal.

As kids we didn't dwell much on the war, unless something extraordinary happened. The atmosphere in the project at the time wasn't that we were there because of the War, even though that was the case.

I can remember rationing going on. You couldn't go far in a car. You were given gas tickets that allowed you to purchase certain amounts of gas. There were shortages. You couldn't buy butter, or sugar. You were given stamps to buy some foods. We adjusted to that, although I don't think we suffered much.

The big deal in those days was the radio. You don't get the graphics that you do today. We didn't sit down with that part of the newspaper. We kids were interested in the sports! And I think the parents tried to keep you away from it. I remember one time a Japanese sub was found off Long Island. Now that was trauma. Before that, the war was 5,000 miles away.

One time Father Skelley from St. John's (a church serving Charter Oak) asked me if I wanted to caddy. He was a great golfer. I was thrilled that he would asked me! We went to Wethersfield. He gave me the golf bag to look after, which I would have died for before giving it up. He went inside the clubhouse.

Some time passed and this fellow came over in a bright gold outfit and asked me for a club. I said, no way, you're not going to touch this! Turned out it was Father Skelley! I'd never seen him before without the black suit and collar.

What would sum up for me the positive aspect of the project? The kids. If you wanted to play baseball, you had no trouble getting 18 guys. If you wanted to play basketball, it became a farce. You'd have 30 guys and only 10 could play! Kids, upon kids, upon kids! That was fantastic.

My mother was the Democratic captain of the precinct that covered Charter Oak. This was a labor force, which meant that they were substantially Democrat. As a consequence, on election day, Charter Oak was very important. Of 2,000 eligible voters, 1,700 would vote, of those 1,575 went Democratic. All those people close together. You were constantly calling and banging on doors and getting people out.

We never thought of ourselves coming from the project. Anyway, for me, it was a very positive experience. Later, people wanted to hide that they came from the Terrace.

Dan Lynch served as the Chief State Prosecutor in Hartford.

Hartford was placed in a 'dim-out' zone beginning November 30, 1942. The order meant the dimming of all exterior advertising sings, streets lights, and shading of auto headlights by covering upper half of each lens. Why? City lights could serve as beacons for approaching enemy planes. Violators were subject to a $5,000 fine and a year in jail. [22]

Charter Oak's Marilyn Romano remembered the time:

> "It was during the war. We had blackouts. As teenagers we were civil defense workers. We used to go around to make sure everyone's black shades were drawn so there were no lights shining. No one could have a light shining in their house. We had no cellars to run to, so that's why we had black-out shades. All us kids had to put on hardhats."

Dan Lynch remembers:

> "The blackouts provided some anxiety for us. When there were alerts, wardens walked around. If there was light, you were in trouble. No lights were allowed. I used to babysit when I was 12 or 13. I might fall asleep, and the parents might not get back until 10:30. The sirens would go off at ten o'clock, but I didn't hear them because I was asleep, until I woke to hear pounding on the door. They'd say, Hey you're in violation! It was a serious piece of business."

Rallies to raise money through the sale of bonds were a frequent and important local event. One news report said that:

> ". . . 10,000 Americans gathered around the Times Portico last night under the light of floodlamps, and heard that Greater Hartford has already pledged more than $4,000,000 in War Bonds for September 1942.
>
> "In one of the strongest statements ever delivered to a Hartford audience, the motion picture actor, Charles Laughton, veteran of the old Western Front, told them it is not enough if we are to save American boys who are being 'out-machined' by the enemy.
>
> "As for the enemies of the United Nations," Laughton declared "you are helping them by your apathy." Mr. Laughton, Ann Rutherford and Virginia Gilmore pleaded for greater sales

Young Charter Oak friends, Easter 1946. (Left to right): Danny Bellwian, Joe Demaine, Ray Bellwian, Buz Coughlin, and George Eddy Forance.

during a pause in their current tour for the local Caravan of Stars War Bond Rally. [27]

When Charter Oak opened in the 1940s, an American flag hung in almost every window. Later, some windows had gold stars dangling from the sills — an indication that the family had lost a loved one in World War II. [146]

Chapter Five

Charter Oak Neighborhood Grows
1943 to 1960

Throughout the 1940s, Charter Oak continued to develop into a neighborhood, despite limitations of design and location. Trees and grass were planted and maintained by a small paid staff, as well as by residents themselves. In the winter, up to 8 men using shovels would remove snow until a mechanical snow blower was purchased and put into operation in 1951. [85]

Along Newfield Avenue, 1.8 acres were set aside for a shopping center. A supermarket, drugstore, sundries and other shops catering to personal services, including offices for a physician and for a dentist, were proposed in 1943. Ten years later, the Charter Oak shopping center was not yet off the ground. One firm submitted plans, but later withdrew the offer. In 1953, the Authority was still willing to discuss this shopping center with any private developer. In time, a grocery and several other small stores opened in the area. [87]

Other improvements were made to make living easier in Charter Oak. In 1943 a wooden footbridge was erected to span the river, as what was then called the 'D-side' of Charter Oak was cut off by the Park River. Prior to the footbridge, tenants had to make a .75 mile trip to the management office on the 'A-side' of Charter Oak. The bridge was washed out by the flood of 1955, and never replaced.

The community building on Overlook Terrace continued to be a focal point of neighborhood activity. By

Charter Oak lending library at Community Building, May 1948.

1943 it expanded to include a school for three kindergarten classes, run by the Board of Education. These classes transferred to the new Mary Hooker School, which opened near the D-side in April 1952.

(Mary Mather Turner Hooker was the state's first woman legislator (1921 to 1929), a notable philanthropist and a descendant of the city's founder, Thomas Hooker. She also served on the Hartford Board of Education with an interest in the 'academically handicapped'. Mary Hooker died at 75 in 1939. [65])

Housing Needs Continue

Despite the construction of more than 1,700 units of public housing since 1940, as well as an unknown but significant number of private housing units, demand still could not be met. In 1947, a study by the Connecticut State Housing Authority estimated a need for 7,200 additional dwelling units in Hartford. The city had gained nearly 18,000 people, mostly migrant workers for the war industry. [101]

Starting on February 4, 1943 an extension of 152 units to Charter Oak Terrace was built. The Extension, called 'E-side' by some, was constructed within an area bordered by Brookfield Street, Flatbush Avenue,

Basketball game at Charter Oak Community Building. May 1948.

Chandler Street and Sherbrooke Drive (on the current site of the Boy's and Girl's Club, the Capital Community Technical College, and A.I. Prince Technical School). The first family moved into one of the wooden units on January 7, 1944. [48]

Dan Lynch remembers:

> "In the Extension, houses put there were built of compressed paper. They were so shoddy that my brother once threw a baseball through a wall."

Charter Oak Extension was built as temporary housing, but demand was so great it remained standing and was used for rental housing for returning veterans well after the war until 1951. [50] (In the 1990s,

Charter Oak Community Building. March 1955.

there was a general misconception that all of Charter Oak was built as temporary housing. The 1941 Housing Authority annual report states clearly that Charter Oak was built to last 60 years. It is only the Charter Oak Extension that was built as temporary housing.)

Early in 1951, the buildings in Charter Oak Terrace Extension were declared unfit for use and no new tenants were assigned to the project. By June 1951, the area was being vacated. [84] The project was soon boarded up and then demolished.

Little is known of the effect of the demolition on the balance of the Charter Oak community, except for a January 19, 1952 letter from Father Farrell of St. John's Church to Charter Oak's Buz Coughlin, who was serving at the time in the Korean War.

> "The parish has been decimated by the evictions. There's a good number left, and the spirit of the parish still holds."

(One hundred or more Charter Oak residents were thought to have served in Korea. A 'Serviceman's Bulletin' was created to keep those abroad in touch with home events. Father Farrell: "Boys in service as a rule are not much for writing but they do wait for the mail call." Other samples from the newsletter:

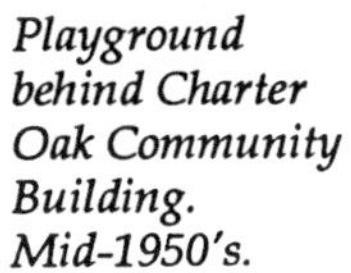

Playground behind Charter Oak Community Building. Mid-1950's.

February 25, 1951
"There was a good crowd attending the Serviceman's Mass on Saturday morning. Nearly 50 stayed behind after Mass to recite the Rosary for Peace. On Tuesday nights the people are praying for the boys in a special way. We're trying real hard not to forget you while you're away."

April 8, 1951
"Tom O'Rourke was home this week sporting the new Air Force uniform. Gee, they certainly make the boys look sharp. The color blue looks so good on most of them. Maybe that's why the Air Force chose the color blue.

"Gil Walton was also home this week. I guess he missed the gang (what's left) so he took a stroll to Garvins to meet all his old pals. Oh yes, Mr. Garvin would like to say hello to all of you G.I.'s, he says he really misses you. It seems like old home week here in the Terrace."

Part of the old Charter Oak Terrace Extension land was sold for construction of the Warburton Community Church in 1954. (One of Warburton's early youth ministers was Andrew Young, later Jimmy Carter's ambassador to the United Nations and Mayor of Atlanta.) [244]

A 'Good Will Boys' Club opened a facility in 1957 on the corner of Chandler Street and Flatbush Avenue. [88] The local Boys' Club was founded in 1860 by Elizabeth Hamersley, Louisa Bushnell and Mary and Alice Goodwin of Hartford. It evolved from "The Dashaway Club" and a desire to keep boys off the streets.

Alumni of Hartford's Southwest Boys' Club include State Senator John Fonfara, boxing champion Willie Pep, and Bloomfield, Connecticut School superintendent Paul Copes. "It was like family," Charter Oak resident Paul Copes said of the Boy's Club. "It was extremely important to me." [115]

Cindy Reaves, whose husband Dana grew up in the nearby Rice Heights housing project in the 1960's described the Boy's Club as the 'heartbeat of the neighborhood'.

Another portion of the Charter Oak land was used for a state-supported regional technical school. [87] The pattern for a statewide system of schools for trade education and technical training was worked out in 1907 by the State. A few years later, in 1910, two schools were opened, one in New Britain, and one in Bridgeport. It was a time when Connecticut industry was growing rapidly and the need for trained personnel was increasing. [30]

In Hartford, the vocational school originally was on Washington Street and was built in 1929 with a capacity for 500 students. The new facility, the Albert I. Prince Technical School, cost $4.7 million and consists of a four-building, twenty-acre campus at 500 Brookfield Street.

The new school doubled the day capacity and can accommodate 3,000 in its evening school, adult education program. It is named after former Hartford Times editorial writer and State Board of Education Chairman Albert I. Prince, who died March 2, 1956. His widow turned the first spadeful of earth at groundbreaking ceremony on March 17, 1959. 'Prince Tech', as it is commonly called, opened on September 19, 1960. [31]

Ron Copes, former Charter Oak resident

I lived in Charter Oak in the 1950's and '60's. We lived at A-112 first, then as the family grew (7 sisters and 5 brothers) we moved to C-67, which in the mid-1960's was renamed 264 Rainbow Road. There were no streets then, just a letter and a number on each house. Before Charter Oak, we lived in Bellevue Square, on Kennedy Street, and on Walnut Street too. We had four bedrooms, and one bathroom — and we made it work!

I spent a lot of time at the community center after school. And the Boy's Club too. I went to Camp Courant quite a bit. For us it was peanut butter and jelly sandwiches. They have gourmet lunches now at camp! We fished a lot, went for walks in the woods. There was a store near the housing authority office called the Market Basket. A guy named Jack ran it, and everyone knew him. On the outside of the store was a wall, and we played stickball against it. The catcher was a square painted on the wall. Shorty Campbell and his wife Jenny ran a convenience store on Newfield, a trailer at the time. We used to go out under a streetlight and copy some of the singing groups of the time. I could never sing. We made our entertainment.

Most people were poor who lived there, but we were all poor so that's all we knew. There was a great sense of family and community there. You were always in and out of everyone's home. This wasn't based on color lines, but on the neighborhood. Charter Oak was integrated when we lived there, but color didn't seem to matter much. There was respect for adults.

I went to Hooker Elementary. In those days we went home for lunch, as there wasn't a cafeteria. I remember that when *Search for Tomorrow* came on the television it was time to go back to school!

When I graduated from Hartford Public High School I wanted to get as far away from Hartford as I could. My world was Charter Oak Terrace or wherever the bus line went. You were constrained by when the bus left, or you had a long walk. At that time I felt joining the Marines would be the answer. My mom encouraged me to go to college. I went there on a football scholarship, took ROTC, and got into the army. On my first tour I enjoyed it, and decided to stay. (In Vietnam, Captain Copes scooped a live grenade from a troop carrier and hurled it an instant before it exploded.) During that time, the mid-1960's, my family bought a home off of Blue Hills Avenue. My parents still live there.

When I got out of the service I went to work for MassMutual in Springfield, Massachusetts, where my wife and I still live. I've been back in Hartford for 18 months since the merger with Traveler's Insurance. Fate brought me back!

Today, Copes is the Director of Community Relations at the MassMutual Insurance company in Hartford.

Jerry Martin, former Charter Oak resident

Gerald Martin was a young boy in the early '50's when his mother and father divorced. He and his two brothers moved with their mother to Charter Oak. Like many they hoped to move out and buy a home. They lived on Admiral Street.

We were very proud of our yards in Charter Oak, with flowers and grass.

We had coal burning furnaces and we had to sift the coals and reburn those that hadn't burned all the way so we could reburn them again. Everyone did that.

We went to the Boy's Club a lot. It was always open. And at the time, where Prince Tech is now, was a woods. We had a nature trail there and played Tarzan swinging across the water on the way to the Boy's Club. It was the same stream that runs behind Mary Hooker school now. Sometimes you'd fall in, other times not. We had great times cutting through the woods, chasing our friends.

When I was in first or second grade I remember being fingerprinted at school. I refused to have it done. The police came in and said they were doing it to keep track of us kids. I thought it was about criminal activity, to keep us on file. I didn't believe it. I thought it was an insult to be fingerprinted. This was in the 1950's.

There were some kids going to Hartford High from Charter Oak that would stick books down in their leather jackets to hide them. It was a culture thing. You didn't want to get caught with books, or show that you studied. Kids would make fun of you. Before that, at Batchelder School, that wasn't so important. We didn't have book bags, so we carried our books with a strap.

We had a church on our side, Warburton. We were very involved there with a youth group made up of kids from both sides of Charter Oak. We traveled a lot, to places I'd never heard of before. There was a link with First Church in West Hartford. They had a program where they'd identify kids in Charter Oak to work with. By that time we were in high school. I got the Birch family, Paul Birch and his wife. They sponsored me, not financially but with advice on how to choose colleges and things like that. I didn't know what college was at the time. They were a real inspiration to me.

I went to Camp Courant as a kid. You'd go out every day, get off the bus. We ran around in the woods and did what we wanted until lunch, then take off again and come back when the bus came to take us home. We tried to find this monster we created, Nature Boy.

(Continued on next page)

(Jerry Martin, Continued from previous page)

Tony Bowen and the Soul Choppers was a big R & B band then from Charter Oak. He played the sax like Junior Walker. James Brown had requested that he travel with him! But he didn't go, got into drugs. They made a record, and I still have it at home. I played the trumpet, but couldn't read music. They were so good. They could play by ear. I never was really in it, didn't have the skills. They asked me to sit out quite a bit, but it was fun to go to their house parties.

I started working when I was 14, with tobacco. I hated that job. But I did it for three years. The smell got into your clothes, and never came out. Then I worked at Channel 3 as a custodian in the summer time. After a couple of years there I worked at the Park and Recreation Department. The director there let me do homework as I was working. He was a real inspiration to allow me to have that time. Others were spending time with their cars, maybe shoplifting downtown. I stayed away from that activity as much as I could. I was slowly being pulled away from the Terrace. You had to make deliberate choices at that age. Fortunately there were a lot of positive things for us to do.

When I told my guidance counselor at Bulkeley that I wanted to be an engineer, he said I should be an auto mechanic. I didn't listen to him, and signed his name to some papers that allowed me to take honors math. That challenge kept me going. I thought more about college. Vietnam was also going on at the time. We heard horror stories about a lot of people from our class who went over and came back weeks later as dead bodies. I got accepted to a couple of colleges.

In time I worked at Hooker School as the Vice Principal, back to the school I had attended as a boy. There were still some families that I knew. This was 1985. It was different. I would drive through Charter Oak to work with some of the families. I had a red pickup truck. Guys would block the road, not let you through. Many were selling drugs at the time. I pulled up to them and waited patiently, because they want you to make some ridiculous move so they can pounce on you. Then they see me and say, 'Hey, it's Mr. Martin. He's cool'. It hurt some to see people you knew doing so badly.

Martin is the principal at Hartford's Rawson Elementary School.

Laura Taylor, Former Charter Oak resident

Everything I remember about my life is from my time in Charter Oak. And if it was anything like it was when I was there, I would raise my children there in a second. It was just a lovely place to be. It was a neighborhood. Lived there in 1957 through 1981, then I bought a house.

It was hard to get into mischief. Because if the Sanders didn't know you, the Hall's knew you, if the Hall's didn't know you the Miller's knew you — everyone knew you. And it was well-integrated. Everyone cared for each other.

As far as teen pregnancy, we hardly had any. We knew there were three girls in Charter Oak at the time who were pregnant. And everybody knew them! And everyone knew all of the drug addicts. And we respected each other. They told us to go home if we wandered into their areas. We knew which families had problems too. My mother Martha always had a houseful of people, in and out, for food and to talk.

There was a Mrs. McClendon. She was the sweetest woman. This woman could cook, and everybody knew it! You'd hang around her house just hoping that she would invite you to dinner. We'd say to each other, 'You stayed last night, it's my turn'! She always had a full course meal. I always wanted her to be my second mother.

There was a garden contest. Near where the Housing Authority office is now is a house where the Carabello's lived. You had to pass it when you went home from school. They had a beautiful garden. And they always won the contest!

Near Golden Age, Sunshine Drive, the older people lived there. We'd sometimes go down to help them dump their trash, and you might earn a dime. They had beautiful roses! It was also called Lover's Lane, because it was so quiet you'd bring a boyfriend or girlfriend there. Nobody bothered you.

It was a good place to get a start and then move on. Maybe a lot of the core families who went on left behind the weaker ones. And a lot of the rules weren't enforced later.

Starting in 1989, Laura helped pull together Charter Oak reunions for those who lived there in the 1950s, 1960s, and 1970s. Upwards of 150 people have attended for a picnic, dinner, and dancing. These events were started by Jeanette Bailey, her sister Karen, and others.

Older Charter Oak residents on ABC-side, July 1960.

Durwin 'Poncho' Taylor, Former Charter Oak resident

I lived in Charter Oak from when I was six until twenty eight. Before that my family lived in what was called the "Bottom," near Liberty Street and an area that is now gone. We moved to Charter Oak in about 1956. It wasn't easy to get into Charter Oak in those days. My mom had to go to City Hall to get in.

We lived first at 42 Delta, then 18 Rainbow, then finally 34 Rainbow Road. We used to have to heat by coal, with a furnace down in the basement. I had to clean it out and stoke it.

As a kid, Camp Courant was a big part of our life. We spent a lot of time at the community center on Overlook Terrace. We'd play basketball or pool, other games. We also went to the Southwest Boy's Club. They played movies every Wednesday night.

I liked Charter Oak because we had grass. And we had to take care of it. We'd get the lawn mower from some of the maintenance people. They'd walk around to make sure the grass was cut, otherwise you'd get a fine. Everyone had to take care of their yard.

Chapter Six

Housing Authority Stumbles 1947-1951

With the end of the war, according to Authority literature, the plan for Charter Oak was to allow present occupants to purchase the housing, and then offer the rest for sale to the general public. It is not clear why this did not happen, but this local decision — along with a key federal one — was a critical factor in the community Charter Oak would become.

War housing status officially ended in December 1946 when President Harry S Truman declared the end of the national emergency. [28] Charter Oak Terrace became a low rent housing project in April 1947, when the Hartford Housing Authority voted to convert it from its war housing status after more than a year's insistence that they do so by the Federal Public Housing Authority. The Authority opened Charter Oak to lower income families reluctantly. There had been a fear that during continued housing shortages in the area, families with higher incomes would not be able to find homes. [28]

After the war, the pent-up demand from the depression and war years produced a suburban housing boom. There is some suggestion that the powerful real estate industry did not want to compete with public housing. Claiming that such housing was the opening wedge of socialism, the industry convinced Congress in 1949 to limit public housing to the very poor. [107]

Many of those who lingered in the project from the 1940s had to move out because their income was above the maximum limits. It caused a dramatic change in the life of Charter Oak.

Now that the war was over, many took their first hard look at the workings and impact of public housing. What they saw were isolated communities, and buildings constructed with materials that were, in less than a decade, beginning to fall apart.

The law creating the public housing program in 1937, reportedly in response to pressures from the powerful lobbying of private developers, required that the housing "not be of elaborate or expensive design or materials, and [that] economy . . . be promoted both in the construction and administration." At first glance, this requirement seems reasonable. Building materials were in short supply during the war. But it took only a quick look at most public housing developments, as early as 1950, to see the discouraging result: often they looked distinctively cheap and rundown. [107]

There was another dramatic event that muddied the image of public housing in Hartford. The teamwork spirit developed through the war period between the Authority, City of Hartford and citizens was broken. A growing feeling had developed on the part of Hartford residents that the business of the Authority was not being properly administered.

In April 1951, Hartford City Manager Carleton F. Sharpe appointed a Board of Inquiry to look into the affairs of the Authority and to report their findings to him. On June 13, 1951 (the same year when Hartford's 600-unit Stowe Village housing project opened), while hearings were in progress, the incumbent Housing Commissioners resigned. On the same day the City Manager appointed a new board.

Immediately after taking office the new Board conducted a detailed study of the administrative practices and organization of the Authority and laid plans for considerable revision of policy and structure. The specific details and outcomes of this study have not been found.

An interim director, Joseph M. Louglin, was hired in 1951. Two years later Daniel Lyons was appointed director. Lyons graduated from Manhattan College, School of Engineering in New York City, and would remain director of the Authority for 24 years. [86]

A relative calm followed the early 1950's tumult. It would be another 15 years before the larger Hartford community would ask what was going on in public housing.

Rice Heights housing project site, 1948. Looking west. Far right is the former Royal Park Typewriter factory, now a Stop and Shop grocery. Center, a fuel tower located in Hartford's Parkville neighborhood.

Chapter Seven

Charter Oak Gets a Neighbor — Rice Heights
1948 to 1960

As early as 1945, there was growing concern over where to put the many veterans returning to Hartford from the war. There were waiting lists at all public housing projects. It was decided that a housing development for veterans would be built on a 25 acre parcel of vacant farmland in southwest Hartford, a short distance north of Charter Oak Terrace. Although this new development and Charter Oak would be physically separate, the lives of those in both projects were often intertwined. [49]

In 1896, on what would later become the site of the veteran's housing project, was the Georgia A. Norton Farm, bordered on one side by land owned by Margaret Allen and on the other by John Allen. The A.G. Woolley Fertilizer Works was nearby.

Little changed on the rolling plot for the next half century. By 1920, much of what was to become Rice Heights was the Manuel and Mary King Dairy Farm. [103] In 1947, John T. Barry owned most of the land, which he sold to the Authority for $1. Another portion was owned by the Martocci family and was sold to the Authority for $10. [211]

On September 9, 1948 at 10 a.m., the first permanent veterans housing in Connecticut was dedicated. Governor James C. Shannon (served 1948 to 1949) and Hartford Mayor Cyril Coleman (served 1948 to 1951) were among the participants. The development was named Rice Heights after Fred Louis Rice who had

Interior of new Rice Heights unit. 1949.

been in construction for 30 years and had given considerable time and attention to perfecting the plans for the 294-family project. [66] Rice was born January 10, 1880 in Moberly, Missouri, came to Hartford in 1918, and in 1926 started his own contracting company. His company constructed many famous buildings including the state capitols in Utah and Oklahoma. Rice died at 73 years old in August 1953. [67]

But even this housing wasn't enough. As with Charter Oak in 1943, an extension was added to Rice Heights. It was finished in 1951 and added 148 units along what was called Pulaski Drive, off Brookfield Street. [51]

Trouble in Rice Heights

On August 19, 1955, the waters of the Cemetery Brook rose to heights of more than five feet, flooding the first floors of some apartments in Rice Heights. With police help 66 families were moved out. Damage to the apartments was extensive.

"The floors were like waves in the ocean," Emil Tramonte, maintenance superintendent, said on September 27, 1955. Some 42,000 feet of flooring had to be ripped out. All of the tenant's belongings stored in the basements had to be removed. More than 200 truck-

Rice Heights flooded by Cemetery Brook, August 1955.

loads of debris were hauled away by city trucks in what was called 'Operation Cleanup'.

Just prior to the August 1955 flood, the State's Housing Division found the seven year old Rice Heights was already in poor shape. The development received poor marks in eight separate classifications during an inspection. The report was made by J. P. Zamichier, assistant engineer of rental housing, and included the following:

> "I was amazed to discover that the areas around the buildings were allowed to deteriorate to such a deplorable condition as observed," the report states.
>
> "Large areas around buildings are devoid of grass and many seriously eroded spots were observed. In some places it threatens to undermine foundation footings.
>
> "Grounds were littered with paper, broken glass, fruit peelings, and miscellaneous other trash.

Rice Heights residents taken to safety during flood of 1955.

"The area containing Cemetery Brook, encircled by chain link fence, appears to be abandoned, a typical No Man's Land. Erosion appears on the slopes, at both culverts and at the manhole. Rear yards are reminiscent of a carnival after a one-night stand.

"The high percentage of untidy and poorly kept interiors prompts me to suggest that the project manager in making his inspections should insist more firmly that the requirements of the lease be maintained.

"It is apparent that much of the work completed by the roving crews is done in a slipshod manner."

Such conditions existed, the report found, because of a lack of adequate supervision by the responsible authority. Interior inspections should have been done on a yearly schedule by the project manager or his assistant, but there was no record of any having been made since 1952 — over three years earlier.

The 1955 report concluded with an itemization of more than 600 specific items that needed attention. In just seven years, the dream of Rice Heights was already crumbling. With each year that followed, trouble in Rice Heights accelerated. [69]

John Fonfara, former Rice Heights resident

I lived in Rice Heights until I was fifteen, from 1955 to 1970. At the time it was a place for young, working class families just starting out. A lot of teachers, construction workers — all employed. It wasn't that way when we moved. It had changed considerably.

When I was growing up I never thought that I was living in a so-called housing project. That's all I knew. We were just kids.

We lived at 39 Pulaski Drive. There was a hill in the back, and we used to sled down it in the winter. We played baseball constantly in the park. That was my thing.

We had a tremendous rivalry with Charter Oak Terrace. We'd go to the Boy's Club every Friday night to watch the movies. There was always a battle afterwards. There was a chain link fence along Flatbush Avenue that separated Rice Heights territory from Charter Oak. One night they chased us. We practiced what we called the Charter Oak Flip, a way of getting over the fence quicker. You'd put your arms on the top of the fence and flip yourself over. So I was doing that, and a guy from Charter Oak grabbed my legs. I was going to be mincemeat if they pulled me back. I believe it was Donald Chafin, who's now a Hartford Police officer, who lived in Rice Heights and yelled, "Let him go!" And they did. I'll never forget it.

I was such an idealist, even back then (laughs). As a kid I drew a picture and colored in a Smokey the Bear. "Don't cause forest fires." I went up on the Hill and stapled it to a tree. My memory of it was a huge hill, but it's really just a mole hill. Anyway, I hung it up and some kid older than me came along and tore my picture down. It devastated me. I cried like crazy. It was my first excursion into the real world where something didn't go just right.

I had two paper routes when I lived there, one for *The Courant,* one for the *Times.* On Sunday I had to carry both. Once I was trudging through this ice storm, ice on top of snow, early in the morning. I had my big bags for the papers. I fell, and hit my head on the ice. I was woozy. It was six in the morning and half dark, and I'm lying there freezing, ice falling down, and I'm thinking if I get knocked out here, who's going to find me? But it was fun, and I made a few dollars.

I think you could learn something from being poor then,  versus being poor now. Industry was important, not welfare. It was a working environment.

Even though I have such strong memories of Rice Heights, it's another world there now. It's not a happy sight.

John Fonfara is currently a State Senator representing south Hartford.

Dana Reaves, former Rice Heights resident

Our family moved to Rice Heights around 1960. I was about 5 years old then.

It was a beautiful place at the time. When I was 10 or so they started covering a lot of the grass with asphalt. It took away a lot of the places we used to play football. Me, Ernie Scott, Donald Chafin, John Fonfara — all of us played. We did everything together.

We had what I'd guess you'd call a gang. Me, Leon Ball, Michael Shea, Fonfara — we called ourselves the 'Jets' after we had seen 'West Side Story'. I was 'Tony', like the guy in the movie! We really ran the place!

Joe LaPenta ran the Boy's Club, and kept a lot of us in line. He really looked out for us. If you didn't follow his instructions, he kicked you out. Or you couldn't go to the movie on Friday night. Pool, woodworking, checkers, basketball — all kinds of games at the Boy's Club. And kids came from all over. Not just Rice Heights, and Charter Oak, but from the rest of the neighborhood too. The Boy's Club was our fort. We were there all the time.

It was very diverse there. That stuck with us the rest of our lives. I can get along with any people because of my growing up in Rice Heights. There were some prejudices there, but we hardly noticed it.

My dad was a tenor. He sang at night for weddings and other events. He'd practice at home and all the neighbors could hear him. My mom worked in banking for twenty years, and had her own modeling agency. There were many successful people who came from Rice Heights.

When we were leaving Rice Heights in 1967 or so, other parts of the city had riots. There were more racial things going on at the time. I remember once we looked over to Charter Oak Terrace and saw a car on fire! There was nothing going on in Rice Heights.

When we moved to Roosevelt Street (a residential street in South Hartford)in the mid-60's, people were surprised that we had come out of Rice Heights. They couldn't believe I had lived in a project. Some thought we were all gangsters.

We moved out when my parents got divorced. It was a devastating time. My mom moved back to Roosevelt Street, my dad got an apartment. It was a bad time in my life. It was a real turning point for me.

Today, Dana Reaves runs his own payroll company in Hartford.

Ground breaking ceremonies at Fred L. Rice Heights. (L to r) Prentice White, Connecticut State Housing Authority, Fred L. Rice, Connecticut State Housing Authority, James C. Shannon, Governor, State of Connecticut, Berkeley Cox, Connecticut State Housing Authority. September 9, 1948.

Ingred Johnson, former Rice Heights resident

It was like one big happy family. We felt very secure there. It was a great place to grow up in the 1950's. We had a lot of respect for each other.

I lived in Rice Heights from the age of 7 to 19, on Pulaski Drive. My grandmother lived with us. She loved to look out the window all the time. We were planning to leave Rice Heights, to get a house that had a porch. But she died suddenly one night. We were packing up for the move in a month or two. When I left for work, I would leave my baby with my grandmother in bed. One day I went in there and she was leaning sideways on the bed, dead. It was devastating. She was like a mother to me. That was my heart.

At that point I really needed to get out of the project. There were just so many memories, I needed to move on. To this day I can still remember my grandmother looking out the window of Rice Heights, watching people walk or kids play.

Then people started moving out. It didn't feel like a family anymore.

My best friend in Rice Heights was Patty. We lost touch for years, and when I moved to Manchester it turns out she and her children lived just around the corner from us. Now our children have become friends with each other! A small world.

Lucinda Thomas, former Rice Heights resident

Lucinda S. Thomas was born in 1946 in Atlanta, the fifth of eleven children to the Reverend and Mrs. S. J. Simmons. Lucinda's mother died when she was 12, her father when she was 17. [97]

I came from Georgia. I needed a job and came to Hartford and lived at 142 Nelson Street. I was married at the time. Then I moved to 55 Pulaski Drive, B-1. That was in 1964. It was a beautiful place to live. Green grass. You had to have a job and husband, the whole nine yards. We raised our kids there, we cried there, we had fun there.

I was a seamstress. Anything you wanted to wear I could make it. I made a lot of money — coats, jeans — I should have put a patent on some of it. My kids dressed real nice.

I moved into Rice Heights on a Tuesday. Picked up a key, paid for rent, checked the house out. We didn't move in that day because my husband at the time had to go to work. Everything was packed, so we came back Friday night. There was a letter in the door that said we did not clean our garbage in the back hall. We had never even opened that door! Maybe it was the tenant who moved out, but it wasn't me. That pissed me off. From that day on the Hartford Housing Authority caught hell from me as their tenant. Then the project manager came. No invitation, no warning. He wanted to make sure I didn't put holes in the wall. We were told we couldn't have washing machines. I thought he was crazy. I was from the South. People didn't tell others how to live.

So we created this association in Rice Heights because the management wanted to mistreat you, or tell you how you are because you are a dummy. We said, naw, we're not going to have it. We met in units. It was mostly women. I was the secretary and was working at Heublein at the time.

I love a battle, and I'm gonna win them all. I thank the Lord for every day, and hope that whatever I do will benefit somebody.

I used to walk in all of these housing projects, passing out flyers to let people know we were having a meeting. My kids helped me too. We'd take the bus, go downtown and have lunch and then pass out flyers. We said the Tenant Federation would help change living conditions. We started making HUD and contractors accountable. We had a lot of battles then. Dan Lyons was the director [of the Hartford Housing Authority] at the time. We wanted to change him, so we brought in John Wardlaw [Director, 1977]. We organized and had a lot of power.

(Continued on next page)

Rice Heights construction in progress, 1948, looking east.

(Lucinda Thomas, Continued from previous page)

One time the housing authority wouldn't let this woman move into an apartment. At the time Mr. Lyons had a secretary who had been with the City. We wanted to have a meeting. We went to the place with the most roaches, in Stowe Village. We took a soft margarine container, took out all of the margarine and left it open on the counter overnight. We wanted to collect roaches.

We went to the meeting and put it on top of the table. We wanted to give it to the commissioner. The secretary was about 55 and so nosy, that she opened it and started throwing up, again and again. She went out that door and never came back.

People were concerned about one another. Everyone looked out for everybody else's kids. It's not like that anywhere now. It changed because you lost the love for family. People didn't stay on welfare long, there was too much pride. Drugs started moving in and took over. I remember some people who used to be on heroin, but you never knew it because they had too much pride and hid it. They didn't advertise that they were drug addicts. Now it's like a big old wide room. And they don't care.

Thomas is the director of the Hartford Tenant Rights Federation.

Rice Heights construction in progress, 1948, looking east. Note Trinity College chapel to right of center.

Ginger Foster Manns, former Rice Heights resident

We moved to Rice Heights in 1955 or so, having moved there from Bellevue Square (North Hartford housing project). We were in Bellevue in the mid-1940's, at the end of World War Two. We were one of the first families in Bellevue. It was like nothing we had ever seen before.

In Rice Heights, we lived on Brookfield Street, and then Pulaski Drive. The whole neighborhood would get together at times, for picnics and parties. In the summer we'd fix our yards up, plant flowers. We won a garden contest a couple of years. We celebrated many holidays in other people's homes.

I remember one time I was trying to cook some chitlins for the holidays. The neighbors called the fire department! They thought the sewers had backed up! I haven't cooked a chitlin since.

The year we moved to Rice Heights was a great flood [in the 1950's]. Everything got flooded. I had to take my baby twins to my neighbors house on the second floor. The water was just pouring into the hallways and cellars. You could watch the water rising! It was horrible.

There were many happy years there. I moved from Rice Heights in the mid 1960's.

Chapter Eight

Black Experience in Charter Oak, Rice Heights
1950 to 1965

In the 1940's and 1950's, many Hartford citizens looked to public housing as a solution to the problem of discrimination against blacks in private housing. Still, progress for Hartford's blacks came in small, painful steps.

Housing discrimination, according to an August 1956 *Hartford Courant* article,

> "was the last stronghold of prejudice in the urban north, and has deep roots that stem from very basic and eroded soil. The bankers, builders, and brokers in general readily admit the extent and nature of their discrimination. But they are also quick to assert that they are only agents of the people." [234]

This was a handy excuse, but did little to relieve pressures on housing needs.

Factory jobs created by World War II permitted poor blacks to migrate to the Northeast, followed shortly thereafter by a migration of Puerto Ricans to fill jobs in agriculture and manufacturing areas. This migration created great demands on a housing market that had few vacancies. [104]

Prior to the spring of 1951, the Hartford Housing Authority, like most other housing authorities in the country, was active in keeping its black tenants to a minimum. Hartford's Bellevue Square, an all-black, 500 unit project, was the sole exception. At the behest of concerned local groups and their own commissioners, the Authority was careful to avoid clustering of blacks in particular areas of each project. By such a conscious policy, the Authority in the mid-1950s said that "Hartford has avoided negro ghettos and attendant problems in its public housing projects".

To determine who would get an apartment, the Authority used what one commissioner at the time called 'the rule of the seat of the pants' in an attempt to limit the number of blacks allowed in each project. The limitation had been a means to continue the projects as integrated rather than all-black.

The "controlled integration" policy contributed to much longer waits on the part of black applicants than of whites in equal circumstances (539 black families to 283 white families waited as of June 30, 1956). This was because there were fewer total openings for black families; and the turnover among non-whites was seven times less than that of whites.

By the mid 1950's, nearly one in ten of all Hartford residents (16,000) lived in public housing. Charter Oak was filled to capacity with little turnover. Once a family moved into public housing, they stayed an average of four years. By 1956, one third of the City's black population lived in public housing.

In 1956, Authority Commissioner Thomas R. Bodine summed up the situation as a 'terrible dilemma'. He pointed out that "Negroes who live in dreadful slums waited years for a chance to live decently while there are available apartments in public housing projects".

While the Authority wrestled with this policy, slowly but steadily white families were leaving public housing. Charter Oak's white population went from 98.5 percent in June 1951 to 87.2 percent in June 1956. Commissioners felt that the real reason many white families moved out of the projects was because of the integration of the black family in public housing.

In 1956, The Rev. Eugene R. Wolfe questioned whether the large number of white families moving out might be because they were able to get out and that the blacks had to stay. [233] Lower income blacks had few housing choices at the time. Demand among Hartford's black population for private middle-income homes was high, but the supply was very limited. Large portions, if not all, of the newly developed suburban tracts were closed to blacks. [234]

Despite some objections, the Authority maintained the policy of controlled integration through 1965. Several local civil rights leaders became more vocal in their opposition to the policy. And on March 1, 1965, City Manager Elisha C. Freedman, in a letter to the Hartford City Council, asked two questions:

1. Is it morally right to deny housing to people in need when vacancies exist?; and,

2. Is it better to let people wait for public housing if the waiting is an unintentional by-product of a policy designed to preserve interracial living in projects?

Keep or abolish the policy? The City Manager was troubled that getting rid of it would make it difficult to 'advocate a system of racial balance' in the school system. A decision by the Authority to change the policy might make difficult any plans by the school board and city for neighborhood integration. [77] By the end of the year, the policy was abandoned. It had allowed some success for integration but had prevented many families from accessing more affordable housing. Partial integration in public housing helped Hartford's grammar schools become somewhat integrated after 1946, when only three schools had black pupils. By 1964, all city schools but Kennelly and Burns schools had black students. [235] Without public housing, integration of public schools would have taken much longer to achieve.

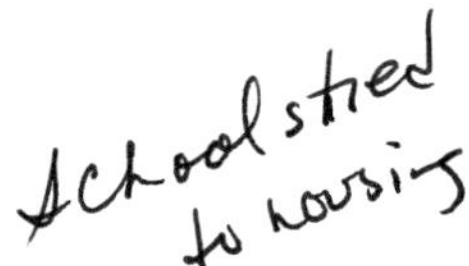

Chapter Nine

Puerto Rican Migration to Hartford and Housing Projects 1950's

"Mostly every Puerto Rican that is in Hartford is connected one way or the other with Charter Oak Terrace. Most of us have had friends or family who have lived here."
— Juan Colon, Hartford Housing Authority, 1997

In the 1950's, an additional force came to bear on Charter Oak, Rice Heights, and the already tight housing market for non-white families. Beyond the black and white migration to the city for defense jobs, there was a major movement of Puerto Rican families to Connecticut in search of employment.

In 1954, Hartford had a Puerto Rican population of 300 to 500 people. Others came and went during the tobacco and apple harvesting seasons at farms in the nearby fertile Connecticut valley.

Those numbers increased dramatically in a short time. By 1960, there were more than 6,000 Puerto Ricans in the city. Thirty years later, the 1990 United States Census reported more than 60,000. [53]

To appreciate the impact of this migration on Hartford housing and neighborhoods, it is important to know something of the source of this massive movement of people.

Puerto Rico, Agricultural Land

Puerto Rico is a rectangular, hilly, tropical island, 105 miles long and 35 miles wide. The island has one of the world's great climates, year round, with a mean temperature of 76 degrees.

Puerto Ricans of today can be a mixture of the white Spaniards who controlled the island for 400 years, the copper-skinned Taino Indians, the original island inhabitants who were all but annihilated by the colonists, and the black Africans who were brought by the Spaniards to Puerto Rico as slaves. [61]

The exodus of thousands of families from Puerto Rico is tied to the 20th century history of an island with few natural resources and little arable land. It centers on the blessing and curse which has been grown since 1898 — sugar. The crop, in a half a century, became the dominant factor in the economy of more than two million persons living in an area smaller than Connecticut. [55]

Even before the Spanish-American War of 1898, most Puerto Ricans were small farmers or plantation workers who struggled to make a living. After the defeat of the Spanish and with the beginning of United States occupation of the island, the struggle became even harder. The small coffee farmers of the inland mountainous areas of Puerto Rico were not protected by United States tariff laws and could not compete against other coffee producers in the world market.

Other branches of agriculture were even less accessible to most Puerto Ricans, writes Ruth Glasser in her 1997 book *Aqui Me Quedo: Puerto Ricans in Connecticut.* The island's huge sugar industry was increasingly controlled by United States investors. Over the first half of the 20th century, United States sugar companies expanded both their growing and processing operations. This meant that the sugar plantations swallowed up huge tracts of land that had formerly belonged to small farmers. As the big growers used more sophisticated machinery to cultivate, harvest and process the sugar, they also hired fewer and fewer workers. In the years before World War II, sugar made up about 65 percent of the island's exports, used most of the tillable land, and employed only 20 percent of the island's labor force during the peak season.

Farmers displaced by the decline of the coffee plantation and the expansion of the sugar industry onto their lands poured into Puerto Rico's cities. There they were joined by unemployed and under-employed sugar cane plantation workers who suffered during the 'tiempo muerto' (dead time), the six months of the year when there was no work on the sugar plantations.

In response to this situation, Operation Bootstrap, a post-World War II economic development program, was formulated by the Puerto Rican government. It attracted manufacturing concerns, mainly from the United States, with the promise of land, tax breaks and cheap labor. Its sponsors promised economic miracles to solve an increasingly desperate situation. However, the companies that came to Puerto Rico did not provide anywhere near the number of jobs promised. At the same time, the industrialization of the island by such companies continued to swallow up land, displacing farmers and other rural dwellers and workers. A study estimated that Puerto Rico's agricultural labor force declined by 78 percent between 1940 and 1979.

Tobacco Offers Hope for Jobs

The post-World War II era saw many United States citizens employed in factory jobs. Often, these jobs were well-paid and protected by unions that workers had fought decades to win. Agricultural work, on the other hand, was poorly paid, physically strenuous and harder to unionize than industrial work. It became increasingly difficult for growers to find people willing to work on their farms.

In their search for the many workers needed on mainland tobacco farms, recruiters logged many miles on the winding roads of small-town and rural Puerto Rico. Cars with bullhorns cut into the sound of nature, squawking the promise of good jobs for those who wanted them. Leaflets spread around the island and advertisements in newspapers held the same enticing message. [236] This effort and the force of the hopeless economics on the island propelled thousands of Puerto Rican families to the Northeast, including Connecticut and Hartford.

"If there's a harvest, you've got Puerto Ricans working there," observed Néstor Morales. Morales first came to Connecticut in the 1950's from his native Cataño to work on a tobacco farm.

Morales didn't know where he would be going until he was on the plane. "You put yourself in those positions, you don't know where they're going to send you," he said. "It could be Florida, it could be Chicago, it could be New Jersey. I wound up in Connecticut." But, Morales added, he and the other men selected were so desperate that "we didn't care where they sent us to. We just wanted to work." [236]

Wages on tobacco farms were 80 cents an hour in 1955. After paying to live in a labor camp owned by the growers, one farmer said he cleared about $31 a week, a full $50 less than the average wage in Connecticut at the time. The season extended from May to November, the working day beginning at 6 a.m. [62]

Of migrant help, one grower said at the time, "If it weren't for this migrant labor we'd be out of business." [52]

Reactions to New Puerto Rican Residents

"We see ourselves as American citizens, we don't see ourselves as immigrants. I am an American with a Puerto Rican ancestry." [158]

— Carmen Rodriguez,
Hartford resident, 1992

Unlike earlier ethnic arrivals such as the Irish and Italians, Puerto Ricans are United States citizens by birth and thus are not restricted by entrance requirements or quotas. Puerto Ricans were granted U.S. citizenship in 1917. They are subject to some U.S. laws and not others, can pass freely between the mainland and the island and are able to participate in selected federal programs such as food stamps, welfare and Social Security. They can be and have been drafted by the military. [158] But since their migration in the mid-1950's, they have encountered a majority population that is often hostile.

Gilberto Camacho, the commonwealth of Puerto Rico's Connecticut representative in the 1960's, explained that many Puerto Ricans migrating to the area were 'hill people' who had little experience with city living. He suggested a series of workshops for policemen who apparently didn't understand the new Hartford residents.

He pointed out that it was a custom in Puerto Rico for neighbors to gather in front of the house and laugh, talk loudly and discuss politics and the weather. He noted this practice sometimes brought a charge of disturbing the peace or loitering. [59]

A 1950's guide printed in Spanish by the Council of Churches for arriving Puerto Ricans gives some indication of the changes they were expected to make:

"Here it is not considered good taste to comment favorably or unfavorably about the looks of the girls that pass by in the street."

"We have wind and snow in winter . . . we have to dress in warm clothes and use boots." [57]

Hartford Housing and Puerto Ricans

Very few of the first Puerto Ricans to Hartford lived in the city's public housing. The Authority reported that only five Puerto Rican families lived in Hartford projects by 1954.

Many of the Puerto Ricans who first came to Hartford settled in the Clay Hill "Tunnel" area of northern Hartford, a neighborhood of older housing bounded by railroad lines and major transportation routes. As the population grew and people were displaced by urban renewal and highway construction in the North End, many Puerto Ricans spread out to the South Green area, on the southern edge of downtown.

By 1965, after the Authority had dropped its system of controlled integration that "limited the number of negroes and 'other' occupants", there were 168 Puerto Rican families living in public housing projects. [78]

By the late 1960's, Puerto Rican residents had replaced the South Green neighborhood's Irish, Italians, Poles and Jews. But by 1973 the city Redevelopment Agency had acquired a great deal of property in the area and began to relocate Puerto Ricans and other residents. Puerto Ricans moved from South Green, not without protest, and joined others in Charter Oak and an area known as Frog Hollow in the center of Hartford. The move wasn't easy. In Frog Hollow, they met resistance from a group of long-standing white residents. [236]

More and more Puerto Rican families moved into public housing. By June 1978, about 57 percent of the 5,000 Charter Oak residents were Puerto Rican. [40]

Chapter Ten

Edges Fray in Public Housing
1965 to 1979

"Many people in Hartford see Charter Oak as a lost community, structurally deteriorated to the point of being unsuitable for refurbishing. These forces have advocated demolition as the only alternative. Life in Charter Oak is characterized by high unemployment, limited medical assistance, restricted transportation, a large high school dropout rate, overcrowded housing stock, no recreational facilities and a general isolation from the mainstream of the Hartford community."

— quote from $10 million Authority application to HUD, 1978

According to the Center for Community Change in Washington, D.C., by the late 1960's a combination of Federal housing policy and local indifference led to a rapid decline in the conditions of public housing. These changes meant that those living in public housing became increasingly isolated, both in terms of income and race. [107]

In 1969, Congress required that public housing residents pay only 25 percent of their minimal incomes for rent. This led to the need for larger and larger "operating subsidies" (money for running the daily operations of public housing), which was money that could not be spent on rebuilding deteriorating developments or building new public housing.

Even in the early days, when incoming rental payments exceeded operating costs, public housing authorities were not allowed to build up big reserves.

Consequently, when it came time for big repairs or major rehabilitation, they didn't have enough money. The energy crisis of the 1970's also hit public housing hard, greatly increasing operating costs. The result was that housing projects like Charter Oak literally fell apart.

In an almost desperate letter, Thomas R. Bodine, Chairman of the Hartford Housing Authority, wrote in 1972:

> "All of our efforts to try to improve the lot of the 15,000 poor people living in public housing in Hartford are being swept away by an over-

Arthur Anderson, President, Imagineers

(Anderson is the local administrator of the federal Section 8 rental subsidy program. He describes an important change in Hartford housing policy in the mid-1970s, the federal Section 8 program.)

I was born in West Hartford, just a block from Charter Oak Terrace on Flatbush Avenue. I've been working in Hartford since 1972.

Section 8 was political. When HUD announced money, housing authorities got existing housing money. But the real money was with rehab — that went to the developers. It was clear to Nick Carbone [Hartford Deputy Mayor] in the early 1970's that rehab wasn't the most important thing for Hartford. HUD had rules against using new construction money in areas impacted by poverty or race. There aren't many census tracks in Hartford that weren't impacted. Hartford wasn't to get much new construction money. Politically connected developers got that money. Nick said, no way, we want those dollars. We can do it without being political, and we can get the job done.

Usually the housing authority would get this money. Nick said let's form the public housing corporation [Imagineers], and we'll run the program. At that time, before Wardlaw, the housing authority wasn't doing such a good job. The City had no confidence in the housing authority. The Authority was in transition, and the City said you have enough to do. So the City took Section 8 from the Housing Authority. We run it to this day.

From time to time the Housing Authority says they'd like to run Section 8. But landlords would rather deal with us. We get high marks, because we have a different motive — profit. And we make money. And housing authorities say they lose money on Section 8. Why would they want Section 8? Power.

whelming tide of adverse decisions out of Washington and the State Capitol.

"In December 1971, Congress extended to Welfare tenants the rule that no family in the Federal low-rent program need pay more than 25% of its income in rent, a landmark humanitarian decision. Money was appropriated to cover the huge loss in rental incomes, but the President impounded much of it and then also cut back regular operating subsidies.

"This cost the Hartford Housing Authority over $1 million, wiping out our slender reserves. We've had to make drastic cutbacks in services to all our tenants.

"Apparently the needs of the poor don't have a high priority in America." [95]

Nick Carbone, former Hartford Deputy Mayor

Carbone describes how controlling Section 8 funding affected housing rehabilitation in Hartford.

Section 8 program started in the 70's under President Nixon. Section 8s allocated for new construction were going to private development. In Hartford [1970's], we had a lot of poor people living in private housing. The welfare then assumed that people lived in public housing. So welfare didn't cover what people needed to pay the rent in private housing. We pushed for an increase in welfare, and also worked to get a revaluation of property to help lower the taxes and stop some of the abandonment that was going on. And we passed a resolution that said there would be no new Section 8 construction in the city. We traded in these new construction Section 8 monies for what was called Rehabilitation and Existing Housing. This helped the landlord maintain the property.

Then we created a public housing corporation [Imagineers] to administer that, because we knew the public bureaucracy — City Hall, the housing authority — was incapable of doing anything creative. HUD said you could designate your housing authority, the city housing department, or a non-profit. A non-profit could hire and fire people, they can get the program up and running in two months, and if they weren't doing it right we could cancel the contract.

I think the strategy worked. The abandonment stopped.

Some examples of the deterioration was reported by *The Hartford Courant* in April 1974:

> "Francisco Torres says that in the last few months, he has killed at least a half-dozen rats in the Rice Heights apartment he shares with his wife and 4 children.
>
> "The toilet in Lucinda Thomas's bathroom has been slowly sinking into the floor. Last year, the pipes under her kitchen sink burst, spewing forth a stream of water with the force of a fire hose, knocking over her young son.
>
> "Earlie Powell, the head of the Rice Heights Tenants Association, warned that if the Authority doesn't take some concrete steps toward remedying the problems soon, that residents will retaliate with a rent strike later this spring.
>
> "The rats live better than we do," said Powell. " They come into our homes and keep warm and they eat our food." [70]

The following is another example of resident frustration with lack of maintenance.

In September 1976, Charter Oak frustrated residents organized and confronted Hartford Health Director Norman Chaucer. He was briefly encircled by a group of tenants protesting rat problems. They confronted Chaucer at his office on Coventry Street with a box of dead rats. [35] Tenant Mattie Bell says the first shot in the battle came on the heels of an incident in which a rat crawled into a 14-year-old girl's bed while she was sleeping and bit her on the stomach. Narcisco Texidor, a 22-year-old resident elected President of the Tenant's Association, told a reporter some of the unconventional methods residents have used to rid the place of rats, such as the cement poured over rat holes and the smoke bombs shoved down them. (The dominant rat in Charter Oak was the Norway rat. It can gnaw through materials as tough as cinderblocks, can tread water for days, fit through an opening the size of a quarter and leap three feet in the air. Each litter can contain up to 22 offspring. A rat that strays into another colony's territory is promptly killed and eaten.)

In early October 1978, Rev. Paul M. Ritter of nearby Warburton Community Church led his congregation into the street after Sunday morning services to threaten a 'rat day'. Unless officials did something about the problem, he threatened, he would direct his legions to collect a bushel of live rats every day for 10 days, and then let them loose in the federal building downtown. It worked. The day before they were to be set free, HUD pledged $1 million for rat control and other improvements. [44] This $1 million would go towards the renovation of 40 units in Charter Oak, which had not been repaired since they were built in 1941. The money was good news, but by then the project had become a symbol of the ills of public housing and the target of repeated protests by community and tenant groups. [37]

Nick Carbone, former Deputy Mayor, City of Hartford, 1970s

Carbone remembers the events leading to the hiring of new Authority director John Wardlaw.

During the 1970's, there was a scarcity of low-income housing in the region. This would deter integration of the suburbs. Our position was, what can we do to get the suburban communities to do integration? We did some lawsuits at the time around some federal block grant monies to force the issue. This is the context in which we ran public housing.

We had an obligation to enhance the maintenance of public housing in the city. The public housing authority was to help transition people from public housing. That effort was breaking down. It was looked at as an asylum. Public housing had to be part of a larger picture. We wanted to take a fresh approach.

We lobbied the City Manager to have Chuck Mokrisky, who was an attorney at Day, Berry and Howard in Hartford to become a member of the Housing Authority board. When Dan Lyons retired, it was an opportunity to bring a non-housing perspective to public housing. Mokrisky came to me and talked to me about John Wardlaw, who was working with the Hartford Institute for Criminal Justice on juvenile justice issues. I knew of him. I had seen him play football, and bumped into him working out at the YMCA. He was given high marks for his diligence and integrity. Even though he had no housing experience, we were so frustrated with what had taken place that it was worth the risk to take a non-traditional housing person and putting him in charge.

By 1977, when long-time Authority director Daniel Lyons retired, Charter Oak could no longer be saved. After years of few significant improvements, the question now became, how much longer would it stand? Lyons left a message as worn and tired as the housing he tried to manage:

> "Housing, once new and attractive, now bears the scars occasioned by the passage of time. Physical deterioration due to age, with a big assist from vandalism, plus functional obsolescence render once desirable housing now marginal." [96]

Lyons was replaced by John D. Wardlaw on December 15, 1977.

Lucinda Thomas, a former resident of Rice Heights, remembers when Wardlaw interviewed for the position:

"When I first met John Wardlaw, a lot of people already knew him because of his work in recreation with youth. I didn't know him, and when he came I asked him one question. I thought if he was going to make a difference, you have to deal with people. Anyone can fill out pieces of paper and send it on down the line. I knew Mr. Wardlaw came from a big family, and I figured he got some good whippings when he came up. I came from a family of eleven, so I know. So I asked him how he'd deal with the human side, and he gave a real good answer on how it would be his job to do the best he could to make changes for people.

"Compared to where we've been, he's done a good job. He didn't have any preconceived notions about housing and that helped. We wanted a director that was human, and that's what we got."

More Trouble for Charter Oak and Rice Heights

In 1977, a state grant of $1,397,000 was approved to rehabilitate Rice Heights. Major work was to include the conversion of 16 one-bedroom apartments into 8 three bedroom apartments. Renovations were planned for the kitchens, bathrooms, heating systems, and electrical and plumbing fixtures. New roofs would be installed as well as site work to add additional parking. [71] Work did not begin for another two years.

In May 1978, Wardlaw called Charter Oak "possibly one of the worst housing projects in the Northeast."

Wardlaw said in the previous 17 months there had been about 90 physical attacks on elderly residents of

Lenny Texidor, former Charter Oak resident

I was born in 1961. We moved to Charter Oak in the late 1960's. It was a beautiful place there. You couldn't do something wrong without someone knowing about it. You'd get a spanking on one side of the project, and then by the time you get home they have already heard, so you get another beating! It started turning in 1978 or so.

There were ten of us in my family. Eight graduated high school, four went on to college.

Our gym and playground were at 91 Overlook Terrace. We roller skated there. We played until 8 o'clock, then we went home. Basketball, baseball, football. They were good years.

I've always worked. Started at nine years old with newspapers for ABC side; *The Hartford Courant*. I did it until I went to high school. I loved it. That little extra $20 a week really helped. I had 150 customers. It was tough with the Sunday paper in the winter because you had to put them together separately. My younger brother used to help me. We'd get up at five, put them on sleds, and away we went! I know Charter Oak Terrace like I know my life.

I lived in Charter Oak until I was 25. I work for the Housing Authority now, and I always go back to Charter Oak to talk with the kids to help them out. Many of the kids feel the gangs are their family. They like the attention. The kids can be protected because they're not by themselves. I think 70% of the kids who get into gangs know what they're getting into. They don't want to go out there and work for no $4.25 an hour. They can make $500 a week or more selling drugs. And they can wear the latest styles, sneakers and jeans. Kids won't go to school if they don't have these clothes because others will rank on them.

It's twice as hard for someone coming from a development to make it, especially from a poor family. This environment is tough, so hard to get out of. I thank God that I made it. A lot of my friends are still there. And some of my family too.

the project. "Our old people are at the mercy of our young people. Crime against the elderly is higher here than in any other area of the city," he said.

In 1977, new Authority director John D. Wardlaw said there had been $32,000 in vandalism damage to all Hartford projects, with nearly half of it occurring in Charter Oak. In just several months, more than 200 walls had been plastered with 168 left to do, 41 broken windows replaced, 65 doors replaced, 432 faucets repaired, and 65 fences concealing rat nests were removed. [38]

In June 1978 came the shocking news that four young Puerto Ricans had taken their own lives in Charter Oak. Family problems were cited as a common factor in the deaths, but the frustrations Hispanics faced stemmed from being uprooted from an entirely different environment, said Wardlaw. He also talked about feelings of isolation at the project and the rampant violence, poverty, and vandalism. "People are saying they don't want to live like this anymore", he said.

At the time Wardlaw said the Hartford Housing Authority was the first in the Northeast to apply for and receive federal funds for human services to try to combat alcoholism, crime, drug abuse and other problems. But the $120,000 expected was considered hopelessly inadequate for the city's twelve housing projects. "There is a desperate need for human services," he said, "We have a crisis and we better intervene pretty quickly." [40]

Hope for Charter Oak?

In August 1978, the Authority competed for a $13.9 million federal grant to rehabilitate Charter Oak. The new funds, if awarded, would be coordinated with a $1 million grant the Department of Housing and Urban Development had given the city the year before to renovate 40 units as a result of efforts led by Rev. Paul M. Ritter of Warburton Church.

In the 1970's, Authority officials frequently faulted the federal government for not providing sufficient funding to properly maintain the complex and provide the kinds of social services its residents required.

Authority Board chairperson J. Charles Mokrisky said the "multi-million dollar grant application is a recognition that the entire project, not just a small cluster of units, needs a major overhaul." [41]

United States Congressman William R. Cotter, D-1st District, toured Charter Oak on September 18, 1978 with Wardlaw, Hartford City Councilman Ray Montiero (a former Rice Heights resident), and representatives from the City Manager's office, the Hartford Tenants Rights Federation, and the Charter Oak Tenants Association. He returned to Washington that day. From Washington he reported that he visited a few apartments that had already been rehabilitated and saw others that needed repair.

Cotter said the renovated units were livable and tenants had done an excellent job decorating them. The other apartments, however, with broken plumbing, broken windows and vermin, were places where no human being should live.

In an effort to get the rehabilitation grant approved, Cotter said he had placed telephone calls to officials at the White House and HUD. [42]

Not long after, $10 million of the $13 million requested was approved for renovating all units, including installing new electrical wiring, kitchen cabinets, showers and locks and sanding and refinishing floors. Handball and basketball courts would also be built. [43]

Would Charter Oak Terrace rally?

Nick Carbone, former Deputy Mayor, City of Hartford, 1970s

I believe the Lyons administration had applied for the money. There was a vote coming up in Congress. Some friends of mine in the Carter White House and at HUD, including the HUD secretary Pat Harris, told me they needed Congressman Cotter's vote on an issue. I told them I needed HUD to fund the Charter Oak grant, and if that was possible, I thought I could convince the congressman that the vote on the President's budget was important.

So I went to see the Congressman. He said, if we can get the funding, I'll vote the budget. And that's the story of the funding. It was by accident because someone asked me about a Congressional vote!

John Wardlaw, Executive Director, Hartford Housing Authority

When Wardlaw turned 12, his father gave him a rifle. He used it to hunt food — rabbit, possum, deer, whatever he could find. The Wardlaws lived in the outskirts of Asheville, North Carolina, then a small city, in a five-room house with no electricity or running water. His father, a railroad worker, and mother, a housewife, had 16 children. Wardlaw went to North Carolina Agricultural and Technical State University in Greenville, North Carolina, at the height of sit-ins and related civil rights activities. He earned a degree in sociology. [176]

You see me in suits and ties. Very few people know about the rest of my life. I'm from a family of 16 kids — 10 boys, 6 girls. We lived in a five-room house on some land that was owned by someone else. My father was able to stay there because he worked the land, took care of the livestock and farm of the owner.

I got my first pair of shoes when I was 6-years-old. I wore them to school, but when I got home I had to take those shoes off. My clothing was worn by my older brothers. It was a very difficult young life.

Once I was playing with a slingshot and I accidentally hit the son of the owner of the property in the eye with a rock. That's how I met the owner. He came over to the house, talked to my father, then to me. He asked me if I hit his son in the eye on purpose. The guy wasn't very angry, he just wanted to find out. The kid ended up losing the eye.

The man said I want you to work this off. All of us kids had to work. You come over to my house, cut the grass, trim the hedges. I did that, after school. He later had me come into the house. He had weights, a tennis court. He was very involved in sports.

Then I started caddying at a golf course. The first time I went the caddymaster sent me home. It was a seven mile walk home. This guy drives by, rolls down the window, and asks me why I'm crying. I told him the caddymaster said I was too young to caddy. I got in the car, and it turned out that this guy owned this golf course! My brother and I got a job. I caddied for this man all through school. He taught me how to play golf. He got me involved in sports. He told me, based on my family situation, that I should go for a scholarship, using my physical excellence. I got scholarships in baseball, basketball, and football.

To help him beat his opponents, I had to learn golf. He said he'd be happy to teach me the game. At the time blacks couldn't play on this golf course. So we'd go out late in the afternoon, after he played his 18 holes. We did this for years. And he taught me how to play. I couldn't play on private courses. A black person at the time couldn't get a scholarship for golf. When I was sixteen I had a three handicap. I competed against juniors from Tennessee, Georgia. But I knew I couldn't play it in school.

This brought him and my father together. I think he helped pay off the house. He just turned over the papers to my father one day.

Sports were very important to me. For me to survive I had to maximize my potential in sports. The way I think now is directly related to

Continued on next page

John Wardlaw, Continued from previous page

sports. You can be the best if you are willing to invest in being the best. But you have to invest in yourself, and work harder than anyone else to be the best. The attitude in sports is so connected to your attitude in life. Even when I was playing ball you would study your opponent. You study everything about this guy. His strengths and weaknesses, everything. You know when he's injured, even when he has a headache. Why? Because you're looking for that edge. My life is conditioned on that premise that I learned in childhood, and I apply it to everything I do.

I started off as an athlete. Played ball up in Canada, Canadian Football League. There for two and a half years. Coach Weeb Eubank, who coached the New York Jets at the time, invited me to come down from Canada. I was a wide receiver. The guy there was supposed to retire, but he changed his mind. I stayed for two years. Weeb sent me to the Hartford Knights [a Hartford semi-professional football team] so I could get more playing time.

In 1965 I started working for the YMCA, youth services. I opened the Stowe Village YMCA because I felt the Y should be more visible in the neighborhoods. After I became the Director of the Housing Authority, I also built the building for them to come to the Terrace. So I am not a stranger to public housing.

After I left the YMCA I took over the Upward Bound program, a college prep program for young people on their way to college. A year later I was offered a position in a criminal justice agency [Community Resources for Justice], working with young men and women, first-time offenders. The choice for them was to go to jail, or work with us and avoid time. I found that 90% of our clients came from public housing. There were a few young people I worked with who never went back to court, never had to serve time. Many of those young people, because of the work of our agency, had their lives changed. Some are teachers now, attorneys. I really enjoyed that, found that very interesting.

I was asked to take over the Executive Directorship of this Housing Authority. I didn't apply for this program. I was very happy with my other job. But at the housing authority, there were a lot of troubles and challenges. I agreed to take the job, but only for two years. Then I wanted to go back to my other jobs. Two years passed, another two years, now it's going past twenty!

I don't do a lot of patting on the back. People are supposed to do the best they can. There's not much back-patting in sports. Have you put in everything you need to put in yourself? You are the only one you can depend on. I believe in teamwork, but it starts with you. You have to be the best first, and have to spend the time required to make that happen.

I knew nothing about housing before I came here. Everything I know now I learned while I've been here.

Chapter 11

The Poor Get Poorer
1980's

The timing of millions of dollars dedicated to Charter Oak in the late 1970's couldn't have been better, as it was also when serious problems began taking over the area. Drug dealers started popping up in front of people's homes. Jobs disappeared from Hartford, taking with them many residents' hope for getting that they would soon get out of public housing and into their own homes. At the end of the decade, unemployment was 65 percent in Charter Oak. Furthermore, the apartments in which people were already struggling were falling apart.

One of the more thorough articles on public housing woes of the time came in the *Hartford Advocate* by Bruce Kauffman on October 11, 1978. He wrote that Charter Oak was the:

> "City's best hidden slum for as many as 9,000 people. The project is penned in on one side by the fenced-off Park River, another side by railroad tracks, and by Interstate 84 on another. Charter Oak is 125 acres that look worn, tired, vandalized and dangerous. Its residents, much as many would like to get out, don't venture far from the complex because they don't want to wait for the sporadic bus service to take them away. So they are isolated as much by a lack of transit as by their own poverty. The people there seem to have been cut off, both geographically and economically, from the rest of the life of the city.
>
> "They stay here," continued Kauffman, "because they can't afford the rents anywhere else. Indeed, if you can handle the conditions,

> Charter Oak is about the best rent buy in Hartford, ranging from $50 to $100 a month, utilities included, and are limited to 25 percent of a tenant's income.
>
> "The project was supposed to provide starter homes for the working poor who would save their money and go on to something better. Many did in those days. But today most are not getting out of Charter Oak and, it appears, most are not even 'working poor.' " [44]

Charter Oak residents had become more than just poor by the 1980's. They had become first- and second-generation welfare families. In 1983, 70 percent of Charter Oak residents were unemployed, with 85 percent of households headed by single women. [98] By 1987, income for more than 1,900 Charter Oak families was less than $10,000 a year, well below poverty level.

Despite the problems, almost every Hartford public housing project had a "waiting list." The Authority's list in 1987 had more than 4,500 families. For many, several years would pass before an apartment became vacant. [237, 238]

Throughout the 1980's, the Reagan administration, eager to overhaul the nation's approach to housing the poor, made deep cuts in federal support for new housing units, which brought construction to a standstill. And during this time, support and supervision from HUD for local authorities across the country were as weak as had been the financial resources. According to the Center for Community Change, HUD took a hands-off approach to the management of local authorities. Because there was little accountability, there were fewer limits on the influence of local politics, developers, and those who didn't want change. [107] This accelerated the decline of public housing.

From Good to Bad to Worse

In Hartford, HUD at least was generous with funding for physical improvements to the projects. In August 1981, Charter Oak was one of four projects in America chosen as a model of public housing improvements.

The special designation was unusual given the national feeling at the time about public housing. In cities, few agencies had a lower level of public confidence than the local authorities that administered the program. In the 1980s, housing authorities had come to represent the failure of American urban policy and — at least in the public imagination — the massive waste of taxpayer money. [240]

In Charter Oak, a mammoth $24 million renovation project (including $10 million from 1978) was underway by 1981. The plan called for some physical improvements and for local officials to better coordinate existing social services. If successful, the initiative was expected to make the complex an 'exemplary site' within eighteen months.

But, said Hartford Housing Authority Director John Wardlaw at the time, "unless we develop a comprehensive, cost-efficient, effective human services support system for our tenants, we are not going to protect the taxpayers' heavy investment in Charter Oak Terrace." [74]

These major renovations in Charter Oak were finally completed in July 1987, nine years after the Authority first appealed for federal money. Why did it take so much longer than the original eighteen-month timetable? The reason, said Wardlaw, was that he wanted to involve residents in the overall planning process and construction jobs, and that it took time to do both.

Sadly, because of the extended timetable or perhaps the inevitability of continued decline in Charter Oak, much of this work that had offered so much promise was already crumbling. New siding on some of the remodeled buildings, for example, was quickly stained by graffiti, raising the question then of how long the improvements would last.

In 1981, Charter Oak was chosen as a national model. But fortunes turned quickly and dramatically. It was given the dubious distinction by HUD in 1987 as one of the most distressed and densely populated neighborhoods in the nation.

Hartford had received $40 million over the 10 years ending in 1987, more than any other housing authority in New England. But there was little to show for all of these resources. Was the Hartford Housing Authority squandering the money? According to HUD measures, Hartford's Authority had achieved an adequate record of fiscal management, and to this day is not considered "troubled" by HUD. The widespread and persistent problems that afflicted some of Hartford's projects suggest that solid management was not enough to solve the financial and social ills afflicting urban public housing. [237]

Despite the many horror stories about public housing, the majority of the 1.3 million public housing apartments and houses nationwide are actually in decent shape, with one million people on the waiting list to get in. Two thirds of the developments are less than thirty years old, and on average contain less than 100 units. Only about 6 percent of housing units in the country are considered distressed, according to the 1992 report of the National Commission on Distressed Public Housing. [107]

The Strong Survive

Despite the disintegration of Charter Oak and Rice Heights, many families managed to survive. While residents were obviously not happy about rising crime and violence, many continued to rely on important social support systems located in Charter Oak. Networks of friends and family were extensive, providing invaluable child care assistance, temporary shelter, and friendship. [242]

There may not have been as many success stories in the 1980s and '90s as in the beginning decades of Charter Oak Terrace, but many solid, hardworking people continued to live in Hartford's public housing. Some managed to raise stable families, and some were able to move up and then out of Charter Oak. Some examples:

Lena Roy, former Charter Oak resident, 1980's

I was born and raised in Charter Oak. My father moved there when he was thirteen. My mother grew up in Rice Heights. They met, and moved out when I was sixteen. Later on I moved back to Charter Oak.

We lived on the corner on O'Neil Road. My mother remembers that the windows used to open out. She laughed when kids used to run around the building and smack into the windows!

When I was a kid they used to come out to show movies. They'd have little film projectors, and show the movie on the side of a building. The carnival used to come every year, set up where the basketball court is now. My parents used to keep us real busy. They're still together, thirty five years now.

It was a good area. It was a lot different, and easier for me to be raised there than my children. We called the Mahoney and Newfield area 'Never Never Land' because it was the quiet part of the project. As kids we ran around there a lot. When I got my first apartment I wanted to live in 'Never Never Land'. Everyone looked out for everybody else there. It was the best part of the project. People kept the place clean, picked up glass and trash even if it wasn't their own. No one could do anything without someone knowing.

I was never ashamed that I lived in the project. I sometimes played bingo with my mother, and people who used to live in Charter Oak were shocked that I still lived in Charter Oak. What about the violence? I think that can happen anywhere, even in the most perfect neighborhood. Violence isn't just in the projects, and it bothers me that some people think that.

When we were kids and had arguments, if we had a beef, we'd fight and be friends the next day. Today it's drivebys [shootings]. I have to worry about my boys (ten and fourteen years old) getting jumped. Kids want to prove how tough they are. I tried to be open with my kids. I know a friend of my son's, the gang wanted to take him behind the handball court and beat him up because he wouldn't join. But my kids weren't involved.

I made a good home in Charter Oak, even though the surroundings weren't very good.

Terrell Milner, former Charter Oak resident

I lived in Charter Oak all my life. My mom had been on Delta Street (A-side) for 32 years; she just moved out a year ago. I was on Victory Street eleven years, then Brookfield.

There was fightin' and shootin', but you had your friends. You could sit outside on your porch at times and talk. Way back in the day you could sit out all the time. When it got worse you wished you could move out, but you couldn't afford to, so you just dealt with the situation. After a while you got so immuned to everything that nothing really fazed you.

I have three kids. I worried about my boy being caught up in gangs, but he stayed out. I talked to him all the time. And trusted him to do the right thing. "They crazy," I'd say. "Only thing they do for you is shorten your life." My daughter and son want to go to college. I was blessed in that way. I'm so proud! So much could have gone wrong in that environment.

"You live over there? I don't know how you can do that," people would say when I said I lived in Charter Oak. When you said that you'd always get negatives. It was like Charter Oak was the worst thing in the world.

Faith Barnes, former Charter Oak resident

We moved to Charter Oak in 1970, me, my mom, and my sister. I begged my mother not to move there.

Over time the project grew on me. It became the only place I knew. I lived there for 25 years! I didn't just stay in my house. I got involved in the community. When I saw a contractor come in to do work, I asked for a job, and I got a job. Construction. Even though I'm not in Charter Oak now, I still go back to volunteer. I help out with the Cub Scouts.

My mother struggled. She worked tobacco, but still provided for all 6 of us kids. I saw her, and said that I didn't want to struggle. I got out there, started working. Seven years ago I got off the welfare remember one year my daughter and I were sitting there. I said to her, both of us are on welfare, one of us should get up and work. She went on to college. I got a job, she went to school.

I made it. I have goals to reach. I'm gonna get there, no matter what. I don't understand when people say I came from the project, so I can't do that. You can do anything you want. You can reach your goal. I did it. I have a nice house now, and nice things.

Maria Ayala, former Charter Oak resident

We lived at 262 Newfield. When we first moved there I was two [early 1970's]. We were one of the first Hispanic families in Charter Oak. Everyone else was white. My mom had 11 kids. We had 5 bedrooms. It was nice. The downstairs was the living room, kitchen and a room. Upstairs were 4 bedrooms.

We hung out in the basement a lot. There was a ping-pong table that we played with a lot. We slept outsides in tents sometimes. We would take sheets and put a stick in the ground. We'd take clothespins, break them in half, and nail the corners down. And we slept there.

Our first grade teacher, Miss Atwood, lived right next door to us. Miss Cook was another teacher who lived near us. Miss Atwood always had cats.

Everyone in the project knew us. We didn't lock our doors. My mom had a big rice pot. There was a girl, Tammy, who when my mom cooked rice she would knock on the window. My mom would serve her through the window.

Every Christmas we got on a bus. My dad was a bus driver. Everybody in the project went to Constitution Plaza [in downtown Hartford] to see the lights. That's the first time we'd seen the lights!

We'd play hide and seek in the high grass between the church and the Party Shop (a store that is still there), near the railroad tracks. That was before the church put the park in. We skateboarded there, played stickball too. If you drive over there today you'll still see them playing horseshoes. Mickey, Porky, Lenny, Freddy — everybody.

On the corner of Newfield and Mahoney we had a tree we called Peter. It's not there now. We used to climb way high up, or lie on the ground and look up through the leaves imagining the clouds were different things.

My dad was the neighborhood bootlegger. He sold gin from the basement. He is a little guy that weighs 80 pounds. He drove big Cadillacs. A bottle cost $5. He sold six-packs of beer. He'd go to Springfield to buy it. People knocked on the door at three in the morning, and he'd help them out. He did this until he got arrested. Then the guy next door took over! And he worked for the Housing Authority! Our basement was connected to his by a passageway. When the police came they'd slide the stuff through to the other side. We made some mad money! My dad would give credit. He had a book, and when people got a check they would come and pay. That didn't last long because he didn't want to go to jail, and my mom wasn't going to put up with that.

I wouldn't trade growing up in Charter Oak for anything. I wish Charter Oak could have stayed the way it was. I wish people could see Charter Oak the way it was before.

Aida Maldonado, former Charter Oak resident

I've lived in Charter Oak about 22 years, mostly on Mahoney Drive.

Things began to change in about 1986. I started noticing gangs. I never worried about it before. I saw a lot of people get beat up.

One time I opened my door and saw a guy getting beat up. I just happened to look out. I felt sorry, and wanted to do something. A neighbor came over and said the guys had seen me watch them, and if the cops come they know who called them. I told her to send me the guy who told her that. Tell it to my face. Another time I found out the cops were telling others that I called. I couldn't believe they did that. I don't think the police cared about Charter Oak.

I didn't feel safe. All of my doors had to be closed, my kids couldn't go outside. But we couldn't move out. We just didn't have the income.

Another thing that happened is in the 80's when a young girl got pregnant, the Housing Authority would give her an apartment — eighteen-years-old. They didn't do that before. Now they split the families. Then what happened is that the boyfriend would move in, then his brother, and it became a real mess.

Chapter 12

Gangs Take Over Public Housing
1990's

It's the beginning of the 1990's. Something dramatic is about to happen to Charter Oak. For the first 50 years of its life, Charter Oak appeared in just over 100 news articles in the *Hartford Courant, Hartford Times, Hartford News,* and *Hartford Advocate.* From 1991 through the end of 1997, there were 530 stories on Charter Oak. Why all the attention? Gang violence.

Throughout American history, poor immigrants such as the new Irish, Italian, and Jewish often formed groups in many of the inner-city neighborhoods where they lived. These gangs, which Webster's dictionary defines as "a group of people associated in some way", start as a social, support and safety system for younger people, mostly men, who share a certain background or geographic space. Over time, as the economy and violence have become more severe, the term gang has developed a negative connotation.

Bill Gervais, a local police officer believes:

> "Gangs are for family, protection. They take care of each other. If someone in the family died and they needed a stone for the grave, or to ship a body, they'd sell drugs to raise money. If they only sold candy or did car-washes they'd be wonderful organizations."

As a younger man, even Hartford Housing Authority Director John Wardlaw was in a "gang."

> "Where I grew up in North Carolina, there was the Ku Klux Klan. Being from a big family, living in Klan land, I was brought up in a gang.

> But the gang was my family. We never went anywhere without seven of us. We declared that nothing would ever happen to one of us unless it happened to all of us. The gangs today talk about protecting family. We had to live that way. Even to go the store we had to team up. After school we'd all meet before we went home. We used to practice defense. There were fights."

Early Hartford Gangs

Gangs have been in Hartford and Charter Oak for years. Mike Gorzoch, a former community organizer with the neighborhood organization Hartford Areas Rally Together, recalled that:

> "When I was organizing in Frog Hollow neighborhood in the 1970's we had gangs. We had the 'Savage Nomads' and some others — but they didn't carry guns, and they were almost funny. They were caricatures. They wore combat boots and fatigue pants and tight shirts, and they had beer bellies, and they wore funny hats. You know, they were characters. But they didn't carry guns and shoot people!"

Bob Pawlowski, first publisher of the local community paper the *Southside News* (now *The Hartford News*) had similar recollections:

> "When we first started here there were gangs, like the "Savage Nomads", the "Park Street Posse," people like that. But those guys were like the 'Art Carney' type of gangs. They were just dumb guys and they'd beat somebody."

And former Charter Oak resident Lenny Texidor remembered:

> "I wasn't involved in a gang because our family was so large, we were our own gang! We didn't fight much because my father was a military man and he didn't believe in that. But in the late 1970's we did fight some to protect our neighborhood. No guns or knives, but we fought a lot.
>
> "My first fight I ran home. One of the kids told me to bring some candy to school. I said no. He said if you don't bring candy I'll beat you up. The next day came, I didn't have candy,

> and they started to beat me up but I escaped. That was in the third grade.
>
> "The gangs were very discreet in Charter Oak until the late 1980's. There were just a few guys in some of the big gangs. But they didn't wear colors, and there weren't killings."

Maria Ayala, Charter Oak tenant:

> [In the 1970's] If you fought with someone, it was with your hands. When we walked to school we went in a bunch. I got jumped once after school, and they threw me in front of a van. The van hit me. They said I sold out because I was hanging with some black girls.
>
> The first time I saw someone get shot was down near the Texidor's. The men were playing dice and got into a fight. We were walking back from Shorty's [a store in Charter Oak]. I was in first grade. Somebody got shot right in the face. He was laying there, and the police came. It turned into a riot. We ran home.
>
> There were times when we were in the house and shooting started outside. Our dad would jump on us to keep us away from the window.
>
> My family was in some big fights too. In those days, in early 1980's, everybody wanted to carry a gun. People started getting scared and stopped looking out for each other. People started locking their doors. You didn't want to talk to someone who just moved in because you didn't know what they were like.
>
> Everytime someone died there would be a collection in the neighborhood. The money would go towards the funeral. Whether you knew the family or not, you knew they were from the project.

Hartford Gangs of the 1990's

In the 1990's, Hartford gangs became more than simple social groups. They became highly organized, well-armed, and violent.

Hartford coasted through much of 1991 and 1992 without worrying about widespread gang violence. A campaign in the late 1980's to take gang leaders off the streets had broken up the major gangs, leaving small neighborhood posses to fill the vacuum. There were flashes of violence, but they faded quickly.

But in late 1992 and early 1993, gangs became much more aggressive. In Charter Oak, many more residents than usual were ready for a fight over something. The most trivial slights seemed to touch off violence, one reporter noted: a steely glance, a comment, looking the wrong way at someone else's girlfriend. Fights were also about respect, a commodity treasured in Charter Oak. [118]

Faith Barnes of Charter Oak:

> It's different out there now. When adults saw us doing something they sent us home. Now, the kids stand on the street. My boy is eighteen and hangs with his friends on a corner in Charter Oak and smokes and drinks. It's hard. Some other kids his age sell drugs, because it's fast money. They want those Michael Jordan sneakers. We were just as happy, stepping high and smiling in $2.99 sneakers as kids!

Maria Ayala, Charter Oak tenant:

> When we moved to D-side [in the 1990's] you couldn't run. The gangs said there would be no running because they couldn't be sure who you were. They'd sit on the rooftops with rifles. If it was dark you had to yell out your name so they wouldn't shoot you.

The primary south Hartford gangs of the early 1990's were called the Latin Kings and Los Solidos. Los Solidos members wore red and blue to signify the union of two once powerful youth street gangs, the Savage Nomads and the Ghetto Brothers, which disbanded in the early 1980's when most of their members outgrew gang activity or went to prison. In Charter Oak, D-side became Los Solidos turf. ABC-side came to be controlled by the Latin Kings.

These gangs were largely organized within the Connecticut prison system during the 1980's. When released from jail and returned to Hartford neighborhoods like Charter Oak and Frog Hollow, the gang leadership unleashed a powerful, well-organized operation centered on the trafficking of narcotics and enforced by sophisticated firearms.

City and state law enforcement officials believed Los Solidos, which in Spanish roughly means "The Solid Ones", was establishing itself as the most powerful Hartford gang and growing elsewhere in the state. In 1992, Los Solidos claimed a Hartford membership of about 300.

"This is not a boys' club," Capt. Thomas R. Moore Jr. of the Hartford Police Department's Gang Task Force said. "They are dangerous, well-armed individuals who have a discipline and follow bylaws. They say they are a cultural organization. Nothing could be further from the truth."

Activity often centered around the sale of illegal drugs, such as marijuana, heroin, and crack cocaine. On a good day, reported one article, a 17-year-old could take home $1,000 by selling $10 bags of crack cocaine to his drive-up customers, many of whom came from the suburbs. [178]

Los Solidos gang operated several "gates" in Hartford, drug market operations in the Charter Oak and Stowe Village housing projects. Competitors who did not belong to the Solidos were tolerated on their turf if they paid "rent".[1] [169]

Gang Violence Escalates

Tension was heightened as the two gangs recruited primarily young Hispanic men in the Frog Hollow and Charter Oak neighborhoods. Friends were often at odds because some wore Solidos colors, red and blue, while others put on the yellow and black of the Latin Kings. [123]

Lena Roy, former Charter Oak resident:

> One time they were shooting out there. Everyone is pushing people into houses to get them off the street. My daughter was three. I can see the fire coming out from the end of the gun, and I'm screaming for my daughter to lie down. It was so scary at times.
>
> These gangs are stupid. They're fighting over territory and pitting friends against friends, family against family. When I was growing up it didn't matter what side [of Charter Oak] you

1. The following are warning signs of drug activity, many of which were plain to see in Charter Oak of the 1990s:

- High traffic, brief stops.
- Lookouts, frequently young people.
- Weeknight activity at extremely late hours.
- Expensive vehicles owned by people otherwise associated with a lower standard of living.
- Pagers and cellular phones used by people who have no visible means of support.
- Dramatic drop-off of suspected activity within minutes after police have been called, but before they arrive (may indicate usage of radio scanner, monitoring police bands).
- Motorcycles and bike riders making frequent late night trips. [228]

> lived on. Now you can get beat up if you live on the wrong side.

This tension escalated to violence in 1992. According to the U.S. Department of Justice, Hartford had the fourth highest crime rate in the country, even ahead of Detroit, New York City, and Washington, D.C.

Several examples of the kinds of violence experienced by Charter Oak residents are told in excerpts from the following newspaper articles:

Hartford Courant, October 21, 1992

> "It seemed there was an exchange of words, and one of the individuals fired one shot from the car that struck and killed Jose Morales," said Lt. Gerald A. Kumnick.
>
> Nineteen year old Jose Morales was called "Nike". He was standing with several friends near the corner of Chandler and Ellis Streets.
>
> Dozens of people gathered near the site of the shooting Tuesday, some crying, some discussing every detail of the incident. They all said their neighborhood had become increasingly violent and dangerous, a place where drive-by shootings are common.
>
> Angel Feliciano heard the shot and came running. He remembered seeing Morales lying on the ground. One of Morales' friends was on top of him shaking him, trying to revive him.
>
> "He was just saying, 'No, no.'," Feliciano said. "When I got to him, he looked like he was already gone."
>
> Nike was healthy, but prepared to die. Before he was gunned down, Nike gave his friends precise instructions to bury him in his favorite football team's colors, the Los Angeles Raiders.
>
> Since July 1992 seven other people have been wounded in drive-by shootings in Charter Oak's D-section. [110]

Hartford Courant, June 8, 1993

> A major battle between Hartford's two largest gangs — the Latin Kings and Los Solidos — erupted, turning the streets in and around Frog Hollow south of downtown into a bloody shooting gallery.

Police raced from call to call throughout the afternoon as reports of shots being fired were called in from several areas, including Charter Oak.

Police also chased down reports that gang members were gathering in different parts of the city. The windows of two police cruisers were smashed as officers searched a building at York and Zion streets for weapons. Police recovered a shotgun from the roof. An hour later, they found Molotov cocktails in a building on Broad Street.

The battle is linked to a simmering dispute between the gangs that started several months ago when one gang member beat up another in a fight over a girl.

The two gangs had apparently been trying to keep a lid on the violence, but authorities say tension between the two gangs has been growing in the past few days. [116]

Partial Response to Gang Violence: "Operation Liberty"

"All of the collective public services have failed to significantly impact on the problems occurring in an environment where a disproportionate number of poor reside in highly concentrated areas," wrote the Hartford Housing Authority's John Wardlaw in 1994. He continued:

"Young and teenage single mothers are overwhelmed with and unequipped for parenthood. These conditions present a logical feeder system to the birth and proliferation of gangs in our communities by preying on the inability and unpreparedness of teenage mothers to provide the necessary ingredients in their home for the emotional nourishment of their children. This unrealized need for parenting, generation after generation, is being filled by gangs, some of whom have turned to criminal activities, and some of whom have simply been termed as criminals. In many cases, gang leaders have become the functional parents of many of the third generation of poor in public housing today."[153]

In September 1993, tired of bullets, fear and tragic stories, residents and officials in Hartford said that they would ask the State to send in reinforcements.

Despite a lack of local police union support, neighborhood residents and others pushed for State Police intervention at a neighborhood meeting on September 7, 1993. "We need more resources to win this battle right now," said community organizer Michael Menatian. The City and neighbors forwarded a formal request to Governor Lowell P. Weicker Jr., asking him to dispatch 42 state troopers to Hartford to help quell a battle between the city's two largest gangs. [119]

The role of residents involved in this campaign was critical. A series of neighborhood meetings and actions were organized with support from Hartford Areas Rally Together, also know as HART.[1] These concerned neighborhood leaders would galvanize local, state and federal forces to regain control of city streets.

1. HART was started in 1975 as an organization to build resident power, train neighborhood leaders, and take direct action on specific community issues.

Michael Menatian was a community organizer with HART during the gang violence:

> "The gang stuff, first of all, should have never happened. We were doing a lot, and the city wasn't responding as well as they should have to what was going on. I don't think they knew what was going on as well as they should have. But it happened. That was a do-or-die situation. Either we reclaim the neighborhood or this is it. It's like a decisive battle in the war. I look back at that year and it was like a tour of duty. I mean, people were getting threatened and killed. That's not easy. People like Dorothy Santiago [active neighborhood resident] had two armed policeman in her house with bullet-proof vests, twenty-four hours a day for two days straight. People coming to neighborhood meetings were being told, 'If you go there, we'll shoot you.' This is about as real life as it gets. This is as dangerous as it gets. You had people having their houses burned down. They smashed a HART office window. It was clear that it was us against them. It was that simple."

HART Executive Director Jim Boucher:

> "Everybody in the community was in fear. In June of 1993 I remember folks were sitting

> around thinking, 'Gee whiz, what are we going to do about all these gang shootings?' People are in fear. People are paralyzed. People don't want to come forward. People don't want to attend meetings. A few picked up the spirit by talking about the National Guard. Then we started saying, 'Damn it, why can't we go after other resources that can come into the city and do something about it?' Because at that point, the present city administration was somewhat soft and mellow about all of this. And we really pushed the issue right after that."

Michael Menatian:

> "We had a planning meeting at Christ Lutheran Church with several hundred community residents and the three Chief Executive Officers of the three institutions [Trinity College, Hartford Hospital, and the Institute of Living]. I'll never forget it. We wrote up a mandate. Tom Gerety, the President of Trinity College, signed our mandate that called for State Police officers to come into the community, and if the City and State did not come in, then we would call in the National Guard. This is how bad the problem was, that the institutions would support this kind of drastic action."

After Governor Weicker's decision to send State Troopers to the city was announced at the September 7 meeting, and federal, state and city officials promised to restore peace, hundreds of participants lit candles and marched up Madison Street to Affleck Street, in the heart of a neighborhood where gang members had been shooting at each other since spring. Mothers with children, businessmen in suits and clergy all chanted "Stop the violence" as they marched.

Menatian said the turnout showed "this neighborhood is not lost, and that its residents have not given up. People risked their lives to comes to this meeting tonight." A woman was threatened by a member of the Latin Kings gang on her way to the meeting at the church, he said, but members of the city police Gang Task Force quickly arrested him. [120]

Jim Boucher:

> "There were some groups saying that we were being too militaristic or we weren't being sensi-

Hartford and State Police patrol Frog Hollow neighborhood in the wake of gang violence. Summer 1993.

tive enough to the community. And yet we were having discussions with people in the community who were a hundred percent for this. [Those opposed] tended to be a few people with their own opinions out there — they didn't really have a base. They were just doing that from their own point of view.

"It was a real challenge to HART that night of the big meeting, whether or not there were going to be five people that were going to show up, or if there were going to be more. Traditionally there would be fifty or sixty people that would show up. And after all these shootings, and after all the fear, and after all these massive headlines one would tend to say that people would not come out to a meeting like that because people would be scared of being identified. So how many people showed up?

"Four hundred folks showed up at this meeting, and I think that just shows you what community organizing can do. People do want to have an outlet. They do want to do something. A lot of the time the media and those people who don't represent folks in the public sector throw a bluff on this stuff and suggest that people don't care.

"At the end of the meeting — it's 9 o'clock. Most of the people are ready to get home —

> put their kids to bed or whatever. After the meeting there was a march to that vacant lot that would later become the police substation. And again, how many people were going to walk to that vacant lot? Did anybody know? With candles — several hundred people walked through the neighborhood that probably a few nights before had gun fire." [243]

Operation Liberty, as the police response was called, started with a show of force in Frog Hollow and Charter Oak. State troopers and a beefed-up contingent of City police flooded the neighborhood. Cars were stopped and searched; streets where drugs were sold were targeted for surveillance. In October 1993, a State Police helicopter circled over the Frog Hollow neighborhood, scanning rooftops for hidden weapons. The air surveillance continued through the weekend and City police staffed the department as if it were a weekday. In the first week of Operation Liberty, police made more than 100 arrests.

The results were immediate, reported residents and the local media at the time. As the shooting and fighting ebbed, residents returned to the streets. Business along Frog Hollow's Park Street picked up. Police officers on the beat were greeted with smiles and handshakes. [123]

Michael Menatian:

> "I don't think the gangs expected that kind of response. It was incredible — it was like a ton of bricks fell on them. Lots of media came — German Cable News Network television, CBS — and none of them could believe that the community got themselves organized, and they called out for these drastic measures, and it was working, and the people were thankful.
>
> "The drugs won't disappear. I think it's like a car. You always have to maintain it. I think we overhauled the engine that summer [1993]. Now you've got to maintain that engine. If you abuse it again, or if you don't put oil in it or tune it up, it's going to go bad again." [243]

The initial massive show of force waned a month later in November 1993, and the violence soon resumed.

Hartford Courant, November 25, 1993

George "Coco" Hall never got to eat Thanksgiving dinner.

Instead, he was hooked to a hospital life-support machine on November 25, 1993, his brain damaged by a bullet meant for someone else. Hall died a short time later.

Friends said Hall was a bystander caught in a drive-by shooting meant for members of the Latin Kings gang.

Several hours before George and his family were to sit down to Thanksgiving dinner at his grandmother's house, he went out for a game of pickup football with his buddies. He walked out to meet his friends on Cotswold Street in Charter Oak.

About 1 p.m., George, who had asthma, decided to take a break.

He was standing on the sidewalk, eating Chinese food from a paper plate when a white, four-door Chevrolet Nova with tinted windows drove by. Five youths were in the car, a witness said.

Shots rang out. Police later found eight 9 mm shells.

"It just went bang, bang, bang. It happened quick," said a twenty-year-old woman who had known George since he was a child.

A bullet struck George in the head, and he fell to the ground in front of 239 Cotswold Street.

Blood was coming from his mouth and head, witnesses said, and foam was coming from his mouth.

George grew up in Charter Oak. Friends and family described him as a shy boy who loved Jamaican music, rap music and his pit bull, Precious. He went to Bulkeley High School and shunned gangs, his grandmother said.

His sixty-eight-year-old grandmother Eleanor Hall said, "I can't eat nothing now." A roasted turkey and a pan of stuffing waited in foil wrapping on the stove. A Bible was on a counter nearby. "He was in the wrong place," she said. [126]

Chapter 13

Residents Wrestle with Troubles in Charter Oak
1992 and 1993

"No one person or one entity can take credit for Charter Oak. There were lots of people who contributed blood, sweat and tears."

— Lucinda Thomas
Hartford Tenant Rights Federation, 1997

In 1993, during this period of severe gang violence and in the middle of a severe economic recession, people of all incomes began leaving Hartford.

"Middle-class families are leaving the city in search of new opportunities for both housing and schooling. Those shifts in the market, I don't think we predicted," said School Board member Ted Carroll. [125]

People were also fleeing Charter Oak Terrace.

"We are carrying the highest vacancy rate in the 16 years I have been here heading up this agency," said John Wardlaw. He said the working families were leaving.

"It is some kind of phenomenon that we have not been able to come to grips with. It is having a real impact on the Housing Authority. We have vacant units out there that we cannot control," he said. This compounded the existing problems. As units became vacant, there was an increase in vandalism, squatters, and gang activity.

Gang violence. Severe unemployment. Building deterioration. What could be done about Charter Oak Terrace, and who would lead the charge?

Involvement of Residents: Tenant Association and HART in Charter Oak Terrace

It is an exceptional housing project or inner city neighborhood where residents in any numbers participate in the public decisions that affect their daily lives and communities. In the late 1960's, HUD encouraged the creation of tenant associations to bring people of public housing together around managment, safety and related issues. Success of this well-intentioned idea has been limited over the last three decades. Most low-income public housing residents give attention to more immediate needs, such as food, clothing, employment and care of children. Only a handful join and take leadership roles with tenant associations.

Charter Oak has had a tenant's association for nearly 30 years. The numbers of residents involved, and the success on community issues, has largely depended on the energy and experience of the tenant president, and that person's relationship with the Hartford Housing Authority. Since 1990, Carmen Lozada has served as President of the Charter Oak Terrace Tenant Association. Lozada has led numerous initiatives to bring about an improved Charter Oak in the areas of child care, senior services, public safety and employment training and placement.

While resident involvement would become a key factor to HUD's eventual support of Charter Oak plans, a majority of residents in and around the Terrace were never involved in a meaningful way. Through the early 1990's, most kept informed through newspaper accounts, by way of flyers distributed by the Authority or Charter Oak Tenants Association, or primarily, through gossip.

Surrounding Charter Oak is Hartford's "Behind the Rocks" neighborhood. The central vehicle in this area for resident participation is through a non-profit community organization called Hartford Areas Rally Together. Since the 1970s, HART had not organized much in Charter Oak Terrace, although it fell within the boundaries of HART's target area. There were several reasons for this.

The overwhelming nature of problems was not something HART leadership and staff chose to tackle, even though the often negative effect of the Charter Oak environment on the surrounding Behind the Rocks neighborhood was clear. Additionally, the high turnover of residents in Charter Oak made it difficult to sustain a stable leadership base. Many of those who remained expended much of their energy on meeting basic living needs. And, probably most challenging, the Authority was perceived to exert tremendous and not entirely positive influence over its residents. For example, several residents interviewed said that the Authority would at times give jobs or benefits to promising or outspoken residents in an effort to 'buy them off'.

Paul Capra, Hartford Housing Authority:

> One of the things about Wardlaw is that he tends to keep his critics close to him. He will hire people who may be his most outspoken opponents. Not co-opt them, but gain their insight to understand more about the problem. He has a grapevine that doesn't stop, from his telephone, from visits to his office. The [Hartford Tenants Rights] Federation is used in that way, to get information that may not be all that pleasing. It's another avenue of managing the Housing Authority. Information is key, especially if you have it before anyone else does. It's unbelievable the way he stays in touch with people. I've never seen a CEO stay in touch with as many people on a daily basis as he does. It takes time, but he works sixteen-hour days and it's the only way the Housing Authority can survive.

In 1992, HART leadership became involved with Charter Oak issues, and as much as possible, with the Charter Oak Tenants Association.

John Wardlaw:

> I've always known HART to be there. But what [HART was] about was totally different than what public housing was about. I never understood what HART [and other community groups] were about. They never knew what we were about. When that marriage developed between HART and the Housing Authority, that was a unique thing. HUD created tenant associations. When they developed

> it, it caught on like wildfire. But at the same time it led to isolation from the larger community.
>
> The first one that stepped in to say this is a larger neighborhood was HART. One of the reasons Charter Oak Terrace never worked was because it was isolated from the larger neighborhood. There were times [HART] wouldn't go into the Terrace, or Rice Heights. They'd be doing dynamite work out in the neighborhoods, but nothing in Charter Oak.

The first meeting between HART leaders and Authority Director John Wardlaw took place in September 1992. From notes of the meeting, HART staff and community leaders (including Flora Long, Jackie Maldonado, and Damaris Bolorin) talked directly about community organizing work. From HART staff notes of the meeting:

> "We asked how we could help in Charter Oak, and suggested that we would be most successful if we were the primary strategy developers. Wardlaw talked about the millions spent in Charter Oak, and that not a dent had been made. 'We could have built a whole new community,' he said. We agreed to meet again to detail plans in November." [112]

HART's initial approach to organizing in Charter Oak Terrace was unusual. In most other neighborhood or issue areas, from the start, HART works with residents to create a plan and make demands on the agency that can deliver on those requests. In this case, neighborhood leaders deliberately approached the Director of the Authority first.

It was clear that Wardlaw's 15 years experience and extensive network of relationships in and outside of Charter Oak made meeting with him a logical first step. And, many felt that working in collaboration with the Authority would allow HART leaders time to learn more about public housing while allowing the Authority another opportunity to address resident concerns. In this instance, organizing came to mean a balance of sustaining this unique relationship while at the same time pushing and challenging the Authority to deliver on agreed-to improvements.

Charter Oak residents protest plan to centralize mail delivery. February 1994.

More often than not, HART worked to address specific issues with the Charter Oak Tenants Association. Throughout late 1992 and 1993, HART staff met with and talked with Carmen Lozada, President of the Charter Oak Terrace Tenant's Association, numerous times to share ideas and information. Despite these efforts, tensions were ever-present, as HART and the Tenant Association found it difficult working together, at times competing on similar activities and for the involvement of many of the same residents.

There was also some suspicion of intentions. In a July 1993 meeting, Lozada expressed her fear that everyone was out for themselves and not for the betterment of Charter Oak. She was also concerned about people from outside Charter Oak working in the community. At the same meeting, Wardlaw was supportive, saying that this was the first time in recent history that these groups had come together in Charter Oak, albeit in a shaky alliance. [129]

Lucinda Thomas, Director of the Hartford Tenant Rights Federation, remembers HART's early involvement in Charter Oak:

> "I remember when HART and the Federation fought fist to fist. In the '70's, HART wasn't down there in the housing project. That was when the friction started.
>
> "Then David Radcliffe, [community organizer with HART] came to me [in 1992], asked how we can work together. And Miss Mollie Shelton was on the tenant's association from Smith Towers [public housing; Shelton also served on the HART Board of Directors]. That helped mend a lot of those fences.
>
> "Something good came out of all of it. We could have kept HART out, but we thought they had something to offer to the people. I had never had any objections to that. I just wanted to hear the truth.

Back in Charter Oak, the Tenant Association and HART organizing work continued with mixed results. At one point there were two full-time organizers. Much of the time was spent learning about public housing, building relationships, listening, having meetings with police and the Authority. A survey conducted in late fall of 1993 showed that rats, pit bull dogs, poor lighting, old trash dumpsters, apartment repairs, and crime were issues of most concern. In February 1994, 75 Charter Oak residents successfully protested the U.S. Post Office's plans to centralize mail delivery.

Despite the steady activity and relatively large numbers of residents involved, it was clear that this work wasn't moving Charter Oak anywhere. The larger, underlying issue of unemployment, combined with a living environment that magnified other urban problems, overshadowed any progress in Charter Oak. For there to be any hope for Charter Oak and Rice Heights, something dramatic had to happen.

Carmen Lozada, President of the Charter Oak Terrace Tenant's Association

I moved from Puerto Rico when I was three months old. I lived on Buckingham Street. I came to Charter Oak 13 years ago (1984). I've lived on Golden Age Drive. When I applied to live in Charter Oak, people said 'Oh my god, you're going to go to Charter Oak. They kill people there every day.' So by the time I came here I was so scared. It was really quiet when I moved here. I couldn't understand why people said it was so bad. I didn't know anybody when I moved here. When I came home from work at night I'd get lost. I kept ending up at the wrong house. So the kids tied this big red ribbon to the grill. That's how I found my way home. I never went into the middle of the projects because I always got lost.

When I first moved into Charter Oak we used to sleep outside in chairs. Nobody bothered you. I used to sleep with my front door open, and wake up alive. My neighbors and I used to cook outside, hang out. When they killed "Nike" coming from school, I couldn't take it anymore. We needed to do something. Crime was getting very bad. We had a meeting, and invited Mayor Carrie Saxon Perry and the Chief of Police Ronald Loranger. The only thing the police came real fast for was for an emergency. Nobody would come here. I remember I once saw an elderly man get beat up. They took his wallet and pants. I called the police and do you know they came four hours later? The elderly were the biggest victims, easy pickings.

When Enid Padilla was the president (of the Charter Oak Tenants Association), she didn't really want to do anything. She was more kissy-kissy with the Housing Authority. The tenant office was closed most of the time. We had a lot of problems. She quit when we pushed her to do something. Then we started going to the Housing Authority, making ourselves seen. We keep them on their toes. We made a complaint form for people to fill out if they had a problem. A lot was taken care of because of that.

I used to be scared of John Wardlaw. When I first started [in 1991], I met with Ramon Arroyo and Juan Figueroa [Arroyo and Figueroa served on the Democratic Town Committee and as a State Representative, respectively]. They came to see the place. I was a concerned president, and wanted the best for our people. Nobody really cares about people in public housing. I wanted people to see us as people. So I was showing Juan and Ramon the problems.

Continued on next page

Carmen Lozada, Continued from previous page

So later I go up to see Mr. Wardlaw about an apartment a man wants. I sit in his office and others are there, all looking at me with mean eyes. I said to myself that something is up. They start telling me about everything except the apartment this man wants. I ask what the hell is going on. Wardlaw says, 'What are you running on me, going over there with the state representative and the third district town committee?' He was really telling me off. Then I said, Wait a minute. Isn't it my job to help people in public housing? He said yes, but that I had gone too far.

Then I got home. I was so mad the way he talked to me. I vowed then and there to make him respect me. You're not going to talk to me like that. There was another meeting with my executive board. I told them what happened, and they were very mad. So the next meeting with Wardlaw we went and started to say that he needs to respect us, and that when we tell you about a problem we expect you to do something about it. He thought he was going to scare me, and I was going to stay quiet. I wasn't going to be a little person that he was going to manipulate like he'd done to others. I take my job very seriously. We only wanted our fair share.

Chapter 14

Marcelina Delgado
1994

Hartford Courant, March 25, 1994

> . . . Angel Delgado, his three children and their mother, Maria Gonzalez, were on their way to visit Delgado's mother when a second car pulled alongside Delgado's gray Toyota in front of 71 Overlook Terrace in Charter Oak and somebody opened fire. The driver's side of Delgado's car was struck by several bullets and the driver's window was smashed.
>
> Seven-year old Marcelina Delgado was sitting on her mother's lap in the front seat when she was shot. [134]

Hartford Courant, March 30, 1994

> On March 30, 1994, 100 residents convened by the Charter Oak Terrace Tenants Association pressed city leaders for ways to restore peace in Charter Oak.
>
> Frustrated residents and officials groped for solutions to the gang violence a day after Marcelina Delgado died of a gunshot wound to the head.
>
> Some who sat quietly through the meeting and joined in a march to the shooting scene returned to their apartments with hope.
>
> "One of the things we want in the community is community togetherness," said Christina Huertes. "We can beat them because we don't want them to take our kids. We don't have the weapons but we all got to work together and say what we want." [135]

Throughout early 1994, the Authority and others were actively working on plans that if funded, would bring about dramatic changes in the physical environment of Charter Oak. For many, the shooting and death of young Marcelina Delgado was the last straw. This violent act more than any other pushed those with an interest in the future of Charter Oak to come up with some fast answers. In the next eighteen months, Charter Oak would see a level of attention not seen in most neighborhoods anywhere in the country.

"That was a defining death because it was so random," said U.S. Congresswoman Barbara Kennelly (First District, Democrat). "You can't compare deaths, but hers was a turning point for a city. We went to see [Attorney General] Janet Reno and said, "We've got a crisis on our hands.' When [U.S. Treasury] Secretary Bentsen came, we took him to Charter Oak. Sometimes you have to say 'Help'."

"That's what we told Janet: 'If you can't do it in Hartford, if you can't help us, what do you think you're going to do in Los Angeles or New York City?'" [170]

A week after the Delgado shooting, Congresswoman Barbara Kennelly said she hoped an upcoming visit would impress upon U.S. Treasury Secretary Lloyd Bentsen that Hartford was in need of cooperation from the federal government to tackle its crime problem.

"Hartford, Connecticut is a very, very nice city. It has a great deal to it," Kennelly said. "However, we have a gang problem. We have pleaded our case with Attorney General Janet Reno. We're trying to get one more advocate in Hartford, and say, 'Look, help us.'" [136]

On April 4, 1994, U.S. Treasury Secretary Lloyd Bentsen came to Hartford and promised to help get guns off Hartford streets and out of the hands of gang members. Inside the Charter Oak Terrace YMCA, Bentsen told a crowd of 100 that he would order the Bureau of Alcohol, Tobacco and Firearms to start a joint project with Hartford police to conduct criminal background checks on people who apply for licenses to sell guns in the city. [13]

Area resident Jackie Fongemie:

> Look at when she [Delgado] died. Residents had a march and prayers in her memory. That brought a lot of attention to Charter Oak Terrace. People were hurt, people were angry, people were scared. It brought an awareness, I think, to what was going on. Near that time Lloyd Bensten came and promised help to get rid of gang members. And while he's talking at the YMCA, gang members are in the back snickering. That made me so angry.

In the weeks following the Delgado shooting, law enforcement officials had a difficult time getting information to track down the killers. Many residents were afraid to share what they knew. But in time, the pieces and people of the event began to take shape. Newspaper coverage was extensive. One excerpt of some dramatic courtroom testimony:

Hartford Courant, June 30, 1994

> Police believe Solidos members fired at the Delgado family because they mistook the Delgado gray Toyota for one belonging to a rival Latin King gang member.
>
> A former Los Solidos gang member who said he was kidnapped to keep him from testifying — and who was later jailed to make sure he did — said in court that his nephew admitted shooting seven-year-old Marcelina Delgado.
>
> Ernesto Gonzalez said that a day before he was to testify, he had been taken off the street by four Los Solidos gang members, including one who said Gonzalez had the choice of going for a ride or being shot dead.
>
> "He told me he had gotten permission to do me — in other words to kill me for testifying," Gonzalez said on the witness stand.
>
> "Is there a rule for testifying against a Los Solido?" Assistant State's Attorney Christopher Morano asked.
>
> "Yes," Gonzalez said.
>
> "And what is the penalty for violating that rule?" the prosecutor asked.
>
> "Death," Gonzalez said.
>
> Edgar Montalvo, an 18-year-old Solidos member who glared at Gonzalez during much of

> his testimony, said outside the courtroom that the Solidos have no such rule. [139]

It was learned that gang members who violated Solidos bylaws were submitted to "bounces," timed beatings, usually thirty seconds. "Terminations" were for more serious transgressions, requiring Solidos to be stripped of their colors and banned from the family. "It's like a bounce, but anything goes," gang member Jose Torres said. "You can be hit in the face. Shot. Stabbed. Anything." [199]

Finally, after months of work, came the details of the Marcelina Delgado shooting.

Solidos gang member Pablo Rosado said in court on February 1, 1996 that he and Ralph Moreno were ordered to Charter Oak, where Solidos ran one side and Kings the other. A Solido member was reported to be in trouble.

Rosado drove a red Firebird. In the passenger seat was Moreno, who cradled a semi-automatic Tec-9, one of the weapons covered by Connecticut's ban on assault weapons.

They spotted a car they thought was full of Latin Kings. Rosado pulled the Firebird alongside, and Moreno opened fire. [195]

Joseph Croughwell, Hartford Police Chief

My father lived in Charter Oak Terrace, D-section. He moved in right when it was first built. He was in the Merchant Marine, worked for Colt's. He got a better job in Waterbury, and that's where I was born in 1947.

The first time I was in Charter Oak Terrace was in 1970, and there was a neighborhood dispute. A bunch of women there were teamed up against each other because of something the kids had done. There had to be 60 or 70 of them, and they were pretty much ready to go at it with each other. I had been on the job for three weeks. We get up there, lots of anger. Some had rakes, other things as weapons. Maxi Atwater, who had been on the force a long time, comes out and tries to figure out who the ringleaders of each group are. He brings them together, and has them put their hands on his badge and swear they would stop. And that was the end of it!

Since I've been on the force Charter Oak has been a very active area. For a time we had a two-man patrol stay just on A-side. There was a lot of attention in Charter Oak, although not much interaction with residents. We had more police officers then than we do now.

In Charter Oak you had Solidos, Latin Kings, and 20 Love. When Solidos went looking for Latin Kings that one day they mistook a car and killed Marcelina Delgado. 1994 was a pretty violent year in Charter Oak Terrace. I became Chief at the beginning of that year. We had a lot of help from Federal authorities, and some more funding to hire more officers to get the work done. We also used the resources of the federal and state court system, and with the CORA and RICO statutes we were able to target the leadership of the gang. We've had 55 indictments, 55 convictions. Jorge Pekino [President, Los Solidos] has thirteen life sentences. John Gotti [New York mafia boss] only got seven! We also made sure there were some alternatives to help keep kids out of gangs. The Solidos were responsible for most of the violence.

I had hope in 1994 because I knew what was being planned with the Federal Gang Task Force. We never lost heart because we knew it was going to come to an end soon.

Charter Oak was a significant area in the local drug trade. Because of the easy access with the highway, suburbanites could come and go at will. Most of the crime in that area was driven by the drug trade.

One of the biggest problems we had before it really got violent was that no one believed we had a gang problem. If we had taken a stronger stance then, we might have been able to prevent the gangs from being as organized as they became. The gangs are still there today, though not as visibly. We have to keep the heat on, make sure they get long sentences.

Bill Gervais, local police officer

I was born in Hartford, 641 Park Street, then moved to 26 Ellington Street. I grew up just a block away from Charter Oak! I never left the neighborhood. I got involved with the Boy Scout troop in 1959 and have been doing it ever since.

Lots of kids in Charter Oak, Rice Heights and the whole area — all the Rice Heights kids — went to the same school as us. We all shared the Boy's Club. They always had their own identity. I was more associated with Rice Heights. Sometimes when we'd come out of the Boy's Club, the Charter Oak kids would head down Flatbush. The rest of us would jump over the fence and heave rocks at the Charter Oak Terrace kids. The next day you'd go back and play basketball, do woodworking or whatever.

Gervais said Scouts kept him on the right track. When he completed high school he entered the Navy, and then returned to Hartford where he was sworn in as a police officer in 1977.

My first assignment was a beat in Bellevue Square. Then I went to Unit 2, which was Rice Heights and Charter Oak basically. Then I moved into the Community Service Officer position for this area at the height of the gang violence.

One day they found four bodies [Charter Oak, December 30, 1994]. Two 15-year-olds who I knew. Young people dying was always difficult, especially if you knew them. That was the hardest one for me. I thought it was such a waste. It was during Christmas vacation. I'd taken the Housing Authority van and some kids up to the Basketball Hall of Fame. We're coming back, and get closer to Hartford I turn the radio on. The talk wasn't routine. I knew it was big and in Charter Oak. One of the victims, his three brothers were in the van.

We were coming south so I stopped at the station to see what was going on. The mother of one was in the lobby. The two 15-year-olds were Solidos and were selling drugs. One got robbed. They lured him into the house where they stored weapons and drugs, and strangled him, tied him up, threw him in the closet and took the money. The second kid they lured him in a couple of days later, killed him with a shotgun, tied him up and threw him in the closet.

I guess the bodies were getting kind of ripe, so these killers went to A-side. Something happened, and they killed two more.

In South Windsor when a kid is killed by a car the response is different. Counselors come into the school, psychologists, social workers — the whole day is spent talking about it. Everyone is conscious of the kid who was killed, because they were told about it. Here, these kids witness much of the death and screaming and yelling and the emotion that follows. They see a head wound, a big pool of blood. They know right away about the death. They witness it firsthand. And it is often someone they knew, a friend or family member — and there was no counseling for these kids. The next day these kids would get up, go to school like a regular day. No support. I'd go to the schools and tell the principals about the incident, and make sure they kept an eye on those most affected. Nothing formal in place until more recently.

These kids over the past 5 or 6 years have been taught that the way you deal with your anger is to get even. Retaliation. Violence with violence. There's almost a whole generation who watched these gangs. The kids learn that. You need someone to say that's not right, that's not the real world.

Richie Montanez, Principal, Mary Hooker School

I came to Mary Hooker in 1989. Before that I was at Betances, Kinsella, and Fred D. Wish schools in Hartford.

When I was in college I never thought of being a teacher. I was interested in being a doctor. After I got into college I had a lot of difficulty with math. So for a while I wasn't sure what I wanted to do. I had a group of friends who were studying to be teachers. I tried that, and loved it. I knew that was me. I had found what I wanted to do in life.

I came to Connecticut from Puerto Rico because I got a scholarship from the University of Hartford for my masters. That was more than twenty years ago, and I'm still here! We, my wife and I, were going to go back to Puerto Rico after a year, but we fell in love with New England.

There were 900 kids when I first started here [at Mary Hooker]. Not enough materials, not enough desks or chairs. The staff was and is wonderful, working very hard for the children.

I myself grew up for the first nine years of my life in a housing project in New York City. So I know what it is like. Perceptions are out there that those who live in a project don't work, are on welfare, don't care about their kids, don't care about the conditions they live in, they're on drugs — that's not true. There are problems, yes, but the people shouldn't be blamed alone. We all should be blamed to allow public housing to exist. Who wants to live in a drug and rat infested apartment?

The environment shapes a lot of who you become. We expect kids have slept, but maybe the night before were in a really difficult situation. They're supposed to come to school and shut that off when they walk through the door. That's hard to do. That poses a challenge to the educator, because you want learning to take place but there first needs to be social and emotional support. That often delays the academic progress that can take place.

When we heard about a tragedy in the neighborhood, our school social worker would notify the classroom teacher about the child involved with some incident. The social worker would go into the classroom to talk and listen, or the student would go to him. If one of our students, or former students, had been involved, we always tried to make home visits or even go to funerals.

We had to go about our business during the gang violence. Several times a year we did practice security measures with what we call Code E, when we shut down the school and locked all the doors. If you live in fear you become paralyzed. If that's the case you need to move on. This isn't the place for you.

The law of the land was if you hit me I'll hit you back. Parents said to their kids if someone hits you, you fight back. I don't agree with that, but I don't blame them. This is survival here, and you use survival techniques. It's difficult, too, when a child comes into the school. Here at school we won't allow you to fight. It's hard for them to turn off mommy's rules when they get here. It has gotten better over the years. The number of physical confrontations have decreased dramatically. Why? There are fewer people in the neighborhood. People have space now. If you have a fish tank and put two mice in it, they have enough space to live. If you put twenty in there they get at each other. And some of the people who cause the most trouble are gone.

Mercedes Soto, Staff, LEAP youth program

I was teaching in Puerto Rico, then in New York City and after a while I felt I needed to get back to working in the community. I came to Hartford [in 1994] and talked with LEAP [Leadership, Education and Athletics in Partnership]. I liked the model of youth leadership development working with parents, and children and schools.

I come from a really large family. I was the first to graduate from high school and college. I realized that there wasn't much difference between me and kids who were dropping out of school, except that they didn't have people pulling for them. I felt an obligation to help do that for other kids, to help them reach their potential.

We [LEAP] take a high school student (a junior counselor), match them with a college student (a senior counselor) and provide them with training, everything from child development to how to read with children. We then match the counselors with eight students. Men work with boys, women with girls. We also divide them into age groups, so seven and eight year olds are together, nine to eleven and twelve to fourteen. A year-round program. Now we work with Mary Hooker and Kinsella schools. In the summer, the senior counselors move into a unit in public housing. That helps them understand what the kids feel, and they get to know the parents. If they don't have hot water or witness a shooting, they better experience what the kids go through. We go to museums, parks. We go camping and also take a journey at least 100 miles away from Hartford. The older kids visit a dozen or more colleges in the spring. We're proud that all of our high school students go on to graduate from high school. And we're drawing from the same pool of kids that has a fifty percent dropout rate in the city!

I grew up in an area with drugs and drinking. There was shame then, but not as much as today. So we didn't see it as much as many do now in Charter Oak. Folks do a lot of foul stuff in front of children without even thinking. Our kids are amazingly resilient and intelligent, and they know how to survive. They're still kids. They see adult things, and many have adult responsibilities, but the way they cope with the things they see is the way a child would cope.

The computer learning center we have here is as good as any at any private school. It is very rewarding to see kids come in, full of confidence in using the machines. They help each other too. One time a mom came in to work on a computer, to get familiar with what her kids were doing. A kid there was eight years old, and when the mom asked me for the help the kid volunteered. Let me help her, he said! It was great for him because he was being assertive and helping someone, and good for the mom because she saw if an eight year old can do it, I can too!

It's great to look at plans for the community, but we have to bring folks along to where we are. We can't leave people behind. Everyone has to be part of the community they want to create. I think a lot of the problems are here now because people don't have a vested stake in what goes on here. We're only as strong as our weakest link. If one child or family is in need, then we're all in need. If those needs aren't met, we'll all pay the price.

Chapter 15

Beginning of the End for Charter Oak 1994

Having seen millions spent on social services, safety and physical repairs over the decades, some big-city housing authority officials advocated a new approach to public housing in the late 1980's: the wrecking ball.

In 1987, Bridgeport, Connecticut officials decided to tear down the notoriously crime-infested Father Panik Village, one of the state's greatest public housing disasters. Regarded as a national model of subsidized housing when it was built in 1939, by the 1980's Father Panik Village had become an urban jungle where residents wore bulletproof vests and crack vials littered sidewalks. [138]

In 1935, Father Stephen J. Panik led a five year crusade to rid the area of slums. His church led a petition drive to build the new housing project. Within a year, the drive prompted Bridgeport to become the first ciry in Connecticut to establish a housing authority, with the power to condemn land and build and administer new housing.

Father Panik Village opened in 1940 as the state's first and largest-ever public housing project. It rose from the rubble of 778 slum dwellings.

"The underprivileged shall be known only in history," Congressman Albert E. Austin pronounced at its ground breaking in 1939.

Its first residents were poor laborers who had fought eviction from those same slum dwellings. Soon they numbered 5,400 people, filling the 1,251 units of Father Panik Village.

This small city was built with New Deal money, and it did offer a new deal. Refrigerators. Bathrooms inside the apartments. Hot water. Gas stoves. A mile of benches. Hundreds of trees. A sandlot for children. A community center that even had a library boasting more than 600 children's books.

But in time it became the state's most notorious crime scene — deep in drugs and drenched in blood, wrote one reporter.

The first of its buildings was leveled in 1987, the last unit taken down in late 1994. [151]

Could the same ending come to Charter Oak?

Early Ideas to Demolish Charter Oak

"In the 1970's, it was hard to talk about Charter Oak demolition because we didn't have anywhere for people to go," said Nick Carbone. "No one in the suburbs was going to place low income families. We had to fight classism and racism. The rigidity of the suburban communities was intensified whenever there was talk about demotion."

In June 1978, a communication from Robert Farr, a West Hartford Republican councilman, recommended demolition of some Charter Oak housing units as a means of solving some of that area's problems. The letter met with positive reaction from the Hartford Housing Authority.

J. Charles Mokrisky, the Hartford Housing Authority chairman, said Farr's proposal to demolish some units might require moving displaced Charter Oak residents to West Hartford through the use of federal rental subsidy programs. Farr recommended reducing the number of buildings in the project by as much as forty percent to open up space in the area for recreation and make the project more livable because of its decrease in density.

The letter was sent to the Authority because Farr was concerned with how the housing project was affecting West Hartford neighborhoods nearby. "Communication from West Hartford is encouraging, and steps will be taken to keep that communication open," Mokrisky said. [39] However, there is no evidence to suggest public discussions continued with West Hartford. It would be another thirteen years before the notion of demolition was raised in public.

Through the 1980's any new ideas of significance that trickled out from the Authority were often met with resistance. In 1987, the Authority's Director John Wardlaw was opposed on his plans to offer more social services for public housing residents. Wardlaw remembers:

> Some people tried to stack my board, because there were some opposed to some things I wanted to do. I wanted to get more involved with the social aspects of things, not just focused on brick and mortar. During this time working people were leaving public housing. I saw that coming. I saw the guidelines and regulations begin to weaken. It got to a point where tenants did not have any responsibilities. I wanted to fight some of those changes. So I resigned. I didn't want to be a part of it. That's when the tenants got involved. I guess they took it from there, and I was asked to reconsider, which I did.

In 1991, then-City Manager Gene Shipman suggested tearing down three of Hartford's oldest public housing projects and relocating more than 1,000 families throughout the region. The story appeared on the front page of the *New York Times*.

Shipman encountered strong criticism for suggesting the city 'divest' itself of some of its poor residents, and after sixteen months of controversy — over this and other issues — he was on his way to a job in Philadelphia. [163]

A year later, in a December 1, 1992 article, John Wardlaw wrote that the Authority must look at the reduction of units within a housing complex in order to reduce density, and to develop housing with a mixture of incomes. [114] A good idea, but politics had just squashed the same notion. How could this plan be moved forward?

Charter Oak Team Continues To Coalesce: Mayor Mike Peters

"Either you do things or you don't, and I don't mind putting some chips on the table and letting things fly."
— Mayor Mike Peters, 1995

By the end of 1992, Charter Oak was in a steep decline. But hope was on the horizon, in the form of an unusual alliance.

The group lining up so far for Charter Oak included Carmen Lozada of the Charter Oak Tenants Association, John Wardlaw and staff, and HART leaders and staff. The next important player added to this group came in 1993, when Hartford Mayor Carrie Saxon Perry lost her office to a former firefighter named Mike Peters, who in his first race for public office collected an astounding 85 percent of the vote.

Hartford in 1993 still boasted numerous assets. As the State Capital, more than 21,000 people were employed in government work. The city was also the financial hub of Connecticut, with twelve major insurance companies and more than twenty-five financial and service companies, and several banks. But the boom of the 1980's had not lasted and Hartford was in a deep recession.

Before Peters took office, according to a July 1996 article in *Governing* magazine, Hartford was beset not just by the poverty, disinvestment and social ills of big cities, but also by political back-biting, bad blood between downtown and neighborhood interests, City Hall indifference to the corporate community — and vice versa — and a bitter sense, largely justified, that suburbanites didn't give a hoot what happened inside the city limits. The article continued:

> "Most of the wealth produced in Hartford gets spent elsewhere. Sixty percent of the city's land is off the property-tax rolls, devoted to state government, colleges, hospitals and other nonprofit institutions.
>
> "During the 1980's, as the insurance industry reveled in the growth that gave most of white-collar America its sense of invincibility, Hartford could get away with pretending

> everything was fine. But by the early '90s, with downsizing and mergers beginning to take their toll and retailers shuttering their windows, the city was forced to confront reality: Not only was downtown in decline but its neighborhoods had also long since begun falling apart. Middle-class residents were leaving, while the region's poor, drawn by the city's generous social services, were moving in." [227]

Hartford had become one of the fastest shrinking cities in the country by the early 1990's.

The relationship between Peters and the Authority's Wardlaw was unique for a City and its Housing Authority. Most urban mayors tended to distance themselves from their public housing. Not so in Hartford.

The Charter Oak process forged a public friendship between Wardlaw and Peters, who are bonded by similar urban philosophies, humor and expediency, reported Tom Puleo of the *Hartford Courant.* "Peters supplies the political muscle; Wardlaw the political cover in the minority community."

"We got a lot of people in City Hall with a lot of guts, who care more about this city than their politics," Wardlaw said of Peters.

Peters on Wardlaw: "I love the guy. You're talking about someone who could easily go with status quo and take the paycheck. That's not what he's about." [177]

Others Join the Charter Oak Team

This coalesced local political support for Charter Oak had never happened before. The challenge now was to get the attention of the decision makers and purse-holders in Washington, D.C.

In April 1994, 300 miles from Charter Oak was the annual National People's Action (NPA) conference in Washington, D.C. One of the workshops was on public housing at which the HUD Assistant Secretary for Public Housing Joseph Shuldiner participated.

(Joseph Shuldiner was nominated by President Bill Clinton to be the Assistant Secretary for Public and Indian Housing on June 3, 1993. He was responsible for the management, planning, direction and the policy formulation of all activities concerned with the operations of Public and Indian housing throughout the United States.

Previously, Shuldiner ran the Los Angeles Housing Authority, and was manager of New York City Housing Authority. A graduate of Brandeis University, he also earned a law degree from Columbia University. He began his career as a teacher in the New York City public school system, and then worked as a staff attorney with a Bronx, NY legal services office.) [156]

National People's Action is a loose affiliation of dozens of community action groups from across the country. Each spring NPA hosts a gathering of 1,000 or more residents to make demands on a variety of public and private officials. One notable success as a result of these efforts was the creation of the Community Reinvestment Act in the 1970's.

At the 1994 NPA event, several requests were made to Shuldiner, including one asking him to personally visit ten cities and the respective local community organizations working in public housing. Hartford was one of those cities, even though there wasn't much to show at the time from organizing efforts in public housing. Shuldiner agreed to the visits, so long as each community group personally invited him. [128]

HUD's Joseph Shuldiner Visits Hartford

As soon as the group returned from the NPA event on April 16, 1994, HART extended an invitation to Shuldiner. In early August, Shuldiner replied, committing to an October 18 visit to Hartford. Planning began in earnest for his expected full day trip to Charter Oak.

As plans for the Shuldiner visit progressed, some good news came in on a grant that the Authority had applied for in early 1994. On September 29, 1994 it was announced that the dilapidated Charter Oak Terrace housing project would receive a major face-lift with a $19.8 million federal grant. Under the grant, the largest ever for Hartford's Housing Authority, 44 of the 286 units in the D-section would be eliminated. The rest of the apartments would be enlarged and remodeled to meet modern standards and codes.

Paul Capra, Housing Authority:

> The Clinton administration pushed for 'reinvention' of government in many ways. In Charter Oak, we had not spent any money recently in D-side, and the first big pot of money that came up could, in Hartford, only be applied to D-side. That was one of the requirements for

Mayor Mike Peters

I became a fire fighter in February 1971 and worked at several places in Hartford. I got to Engine Company 15 in 1982. A third of our runs were in Charter Oak Terrace. We went in for dumpster fires, water leaks, car fires, sometimes a building fire. When you went into Charter Oak Terrace or Rice Heights you knew you were going in for something, though you never knew quite what.

It was depressing to go in there. I grew up in Hartford on Campfield Avenue, a three family house. So when you went to a place in Charter Oak you'd see four small rooms, 5 or 6 people living there, the neighborhood a mess, drug and rodent infested, the housing falling down, it didn't make a whole lot of sense. You wondered why people lived there. But most people didn't know how to get out of there. And many people thought it was a nice place to live. I didn't understand the dynamics then. But since then I've learned that it's hard. Dirt poor, not being able to speak the language, not being able to get a job, just trying to survive.

The City really had no policy towards public housing. The attitude was, look, the Housing Authority has it, let them deal with it. I felt very strongly after I became Mayor that we had to address the problems in public housing. I got involved in it right after I got elected. John Wardlaw came to me and said we have an opportunity here. Former Mayors didn't want to do anything about it. But we can take public housing as we know it and wipe it off the face of the earth. Rebuild quality housing. I was very intrigued by that message.

Why run for Mayor or Council if you don't make the changes you want? If you don't do those things, so what do you get? A car? I thought it was so important for residents of public housing that we do something. It is a part of the City of Hartford. It's a big part of our city and directly affected the neighborhoods around it. We had to deal with it.

this funding, that it had to be a development that hadn't had money in it recently.

In years past, when limited capital improvement dollars came to Hartford, the Housing Authority tried to keep everyone happy. So you take in a million dollars and explode it between several different developments. But nothing gets done. It was a necessary political allocation, but had no bang for the buck. We got a new director of modernization, Greg Lickwola, who saw this and said, "this doesn't

John Wardlaw on Mayor Mike Peters:

This agency in the past 15 years has never experienced the cooperation with the city that we have with this administration. I think a lot has to do with a non-politician, a guy who honestly felt for Hartford, and he jumped into a thing that was political, and he didn't even know it. That person was Mike. Very few Mayors in any city in this country have committed as much as ours has. No one comes close to Mike, going to Washington, standing up with me. It was not commonplace what he did. It is absolutely extraordinary what he did. Most stay away from public housing, but not Mike.

When I started here, public housing was heading in the wrong direction. And there was nothing anyone could do about it because of regulations. The more dependent people you had, the more federal money your city could get. Rather than build the city so that it was less dependent on federal dollars, politics at the time created a situation where we would be eligible for more federal dollars to take care of people. That's changed over the past five years.

Mike came in at the perfect time. When HUD was making some changes, the city was changing how it looked at public housing. The business community began to put more money in the city. People don't realize it, and Mike may not realize it, but when he stood up, we were putting in this application at this same time. That made a big, big difference to some in Washington. In time, the Governor and Peter Ellef [then Commissioner of the State's Department of Economic and Community Development] also stepped forward. I think because Mike was first it made it easier for them to get involved. This kind of collaboration is unknown in any part of the country. Mike deserves all the credit. He provided not the technical piece, nor the social piece, but he gave attention to the situation as the Mayor. That may sound simple, but that was a big move.

> make much sense. Why don't we do things a little differently?" So we went after $20 million MROP (Major Reconstruction of Obsolete Projects) for D-side, which allowed us to do all of D-side and to focus larger pools of money for substantial projects like Bellevue Square.

Congresswoman Barbara Kennelly, who helped secure the grant from HUD, believed that improved public housing was important to the city's quality of life.

"A decent place to live is very important, very important to our families," Kennelly said. "Public housing is crowded and we are talking about the rehabilitation of 222 units. It's quite a grant." [140]

Other reports at the time said the plan, still being refined, was one of the most ambitious ever considered in Hartford.

Work continued for the Shuldiner visit. By October, it appeared that a 'master plan' for all of Charter Oak would not come together in time for the Shuldiner visit. While the Authority was somewhat reluctant to push publicly for a plan encompassing all of Charter Oak, they did work discretely on a larger plan. On October 5, 1994, two weeks before Shuldiner came to town, a newspaper article hinted that the Authority indeed had bigger plans for the ABC section of Charter Oak. Wardlaw said he planned to 'cut deeply' into density while using the remaining space and surrounding acreage to locate businesses that could employ tenants.

HUD's Joseph Shuldiner arrived on Tuesday, October 18, 1994 at 9:30 a.m. A van with local HUD and Authority staff and several HART and Charter Oak leaders picked him up at the airport. After a meeting at the local HUD office in Hartford, the group had a 'working lunch' at the Charter Oak YMCA with residents and invited guests.

Leaders asked him to work to identify $25 million for ABC, even though the Authority had not totally finished a plan. At the lunch, Shuldiner stressed the need for broad community support and a sound relocation plan. "We want to get to the point where you make the plan and we fund it. Hopefully I can come up with some ideas — I used to do that before I came to HUD." In a lighter moment, after several requests for funding towards a variety of plans, Shuldiner pulled a check book from his coat pocket.

The $19.8 million grant committed to Charter Oak's D-side three weeks earlier came through a HUD program that prohibited the demolition of units. HUD had been criticized in the past for funneling large sums of money into rehabilitation while reserving less for new construction — for fear that demolished units would go unreplaced and people would end up displaced.

But on his visit to Hartford, Shuldiner said his agency was receptive to waiving the demolition prohibition for Charter Oak D-side as city leaders and the community had viable new construction and relocation plans. Similarly, he said, demolition funds could be available for the remaining sections of the project.

"We are looking to let housing authorities have the flexibility they want," Shuldiner said. "The key is to come up with a plan. If they have the commitment, hopefully we will too."

After lunch there was a press conference in front of the YMCA. "Eventually, the plan is to have all new construction down here," Mayor Mike Peters said. "Look at what we have — 1940's construction, cardboard-like walls. The rats are bigger than the people in some cases. Let's give everyone a quality of life they can be proud of."

U.S. Senator Joseph I. Lieberman and Congresswoman Barbara Kennelly were also among the speakers.

Following the press conference, the group took a walking tour through ABC-side, then drove to D-side for another short walk. After a tour of the city, the group went to St. Lawrence O'Toole Church for HART's largest neighborhood meeting of the year, the 19th annual Community Congress. At the event there were 600 people. Shuldiner spoke at the start, and said that the energy and commitment shown over the course of his day in Hartford was unlike anything he had ever seen before. He was impressed with HART's convening power, and was surprised and excited at the collaborative tone. [157]

Paul Capra, Hartford Housing Authority:

And we can't leave out the neighborhood organization. That was another important star. I think, even before the change in city administration, [HART's involvement] allowed for freer movement of the thought process and planning. The neighborhood group had helped us put together several small grants, and helped to infuse some of the non-Charter Oak Terrace way of thinking into the scene. That the wider neighborhood was comfortable with what was on the drawing board helped clear the way for others to get excited about the plans.

Without the neighborhood group's uncanny reading of situations and ability to penetrate the halls of government and beyond, we would not have gotten the money switched [to allow for demolition in D-side] nor granted to us for [ABC-side of] Charter Oak. I believe that sincerely. The evidence: HART goes to a meeting with cohorts from around the country in Washington; they come back with a scout, which said we can get Joe Shuldiner to come to Hartford. He didn't know where Hartford was before he came here! HART persevered, got him to town. We drive him around. He's bored out of his mind, taking cell calls, asking not to see anymore, but to get the gnat off his back he said he'd do what he could in Washington to encourage people to think about Hartford, and to tell them that they have their act together. The housing and neighborhoods had never cooperated, and Shuldiner said he'd never seen that before. The important thing was that we were working together, that it was not contrived. On the basis of that I'm sure Shuldiner was key to saying that Hartford was worthy of looking at a new way of doing things.

Mary Lou Crane, Regional HUD Director:

HUD's Joe Shuldiner reported to the Secretary about his Hartford visit. I heard his report on one of our Monday conference calls. He was impressed with the degree of collaboration that was taking place. Usually these things take place in isolation. The Authority makes a plan, and then involves residents who may not be happy with the plan. Here the spade work was done up front. It was good to get him to

> Hartford so he could see it. That makes a big difference on how you feel about something.

Concerns with Plan

For the first time since the 1940s, there was hope for Charter Oak. But despite the excitement, some remained skeptical.

Hartford Courant, October 5, 1994

> From Unit 39 in Charter Oak D, the Authority's grand plans seem remote.
>
> Judith Torres, 21, can see at least five boarded-up buildings from her front steps. Many buildings suffer from chipped bricks, warped floors, and obsolete electrical and plumbing fixtures.
>
> "A lot of people here think they won't use the money to fix the place," said Torres. "There are so many empty apartments here." [141]

Hartford City Councilwoman Elizabeth Horton Sheff said on October 19, 1994, that she had serious doubts about current efforts. Horton Sheff said she would monitor the City's involvement in housing efforts.

Barbara Kennelly, United States Congressperson, 1st District, Connecticut

We lived on Cromwell Street in south Hartford, and we often drove by Charter Oak Terrace and Rice Heights to get across town. Later in my life, my children went to Batchelder School. Part of Charter Oak went there too, so my children had many friends and birthday parties back and forth.

Later, my husband Jim ran for the House of Representatives. When he first ran he had a primary against a man named Joe Adilnolfi. It was very competitive, and every vote counted. The two of them went door to door, to every single house, some of them more than once. That's when I got to know the Hardy family. They were very active politically in Charter Oak. I see Betty Hardy to this day! In fact Jim and I are godparents to their son. We have very fond memories of the family. He represented Charter Oak and Rice Heights.

When I was on the Hartford City Council I shared a cubicle with a fellow named Ray Montiero who lived in Rice Heights. He represented what was going on there so well, so I learned quite a bit about the area.

"They have a bricks-and-mortar plan," Horton-Sheff said. "But where's the people plan? Where do the people go? It all looks great and sounds great, but where's the relocation plan?" [142]

Opposition was the exception, however. No one had a better alternative to what was being proposed for Charter Oak. The majority opinion was summed up best by Michael T. McGarry, chairman of the City Council's housing committee, who said in December 1994, "Let's look at this as an historic opportunity - a chance to build some real neighborhoods and give peo-

Greg Lickwola, Hartford Housing Authority

Prior to my position with the Hartford Housing Authority, I served as Construction Administrator for HUD, overseeing the overall development, design, implementation and evaluation of Development and Comprehensive Grants for Public Housing in the Connecticut office.

I started at the Housing Authority in November 1994 to help get the construction plan back on line. It was always John's [Wardlaw] philosophy and vision to redevelop all of the Authority's large family developments so that they are indistinguishable from other housing in the community.

Before my arrival, most of the money was used on rehab, not demolition and rebuilding. HUD rules and regulations were not as flexible. HUD used to say that to get a good performance rating you had to spend the money as you got it. Didn't matter as much how it got spent, just that you spent it.

HUD and Congress got rid of one-for-one replacement and helped give more 'Section 8' certificates for relocations. With Section 8, residents can move just about anywhere. That made it a lot easier to do demolition. [HUD Secretary] Cisneros and the Clinton administration made this possible. They had a goal to knock down 100,000 units of public housing and help revive the inner cities. You take care of public housing, get some jobs and the cities come back.

In 1994, Major Reconstruction of Obsolete Projects (MROP) money came in 1994 for D-side, $19.8 million for rehab. We decided to switch that money to demolish it. It was very innovative at the time, and HUD was very supportive. No one else was doing this in the entire nation.

ple a better way of life. We haven't had such an opportunity since the 1890's." [144]

Chapter 16

Chaos in Charter Oak
February 27, 1995

"You can take the people out of Charter Oak, but you can't take Charter Oak out of the people."
— Maria Ayala, Charter Oak resident, 1997

The mild opposition to changes in Charter Oak beginning in late 1994 grew to a rolling boil by February 1995. Early that month, new plans for Charter Oak's ABC-side were leaked to the press. Beyond a handful of tenants and other neighborhood leaders, most Charter Oak residents had not been involved in the planning process, and when they found out about plans for their neighborhood, they were confused and furious.

Mayor Peters and Housing Authority Director John Wardlaw met with tenants for the first time on February 27, 1995, one week after the controversial plan came to light. The unfunded plan would have razed all of the nearly 700 units, home to some 4,000 families in the ABC-side of Charter Oak, to make room for a commercial development park that would straddle the West Hartford town line.

Both Peters and Wardlaw sought to downplay the plan, calling it a 'concept' still in its infancy. They agreed to set up a committee of Charter Oak tenants and others to further study the idea.

At the heated two-hour meeting convened by the Charter Oak Tenants Association, some leaders of Hartford's Hispanic community called for Wardlaw's resignation, saying he deliberately allowed Charter Oak to deteriorate to justify taking it down.

Carmen Lozada, Charter Oak resident and President of the Charter Oak Tenants Association, remembers the events leading up to the February 27 meeting:

We found out that there was going to be all of this economic development. The Housing Authority had never told us. We had a big meeting [February 27, 1995] and big stink about it. You can't tell us what we need, we said. We wanted them to ask us what we wanted to see. It's our community. I had a lot of calls that day. I heard about it from one of the City Council people. So I called John [Wardlaw] at his house. I was pissed. He said it was a lie, that it was not true.

The next day the shit hit the fan, because it was out in the newspaper. Somebody leaked the information to the newspaper. I'll never forget it. I was at the senior center, and a lady came in with a paper. As I read it I got madder and madder. So I called John again. He said it was a misprint. I said you're not going to do us. You're not going to do us! The newspaper got my feelings, and it became a big stink. The reporter said she was going to talk with the Mayor next about this. I asked her to give him a message. I said, "Tell the Mayor if he wants to do economic development he can dig up his own back yard and do it there."

Well she gave him my message and he called me. I thought it was somebody playing a prank call. He says "This is Mayor Mike." I say, 'Yeah, right" and I hang up the phone. So he calls back again. He asked me if I knew about what was happening. I said no I didn't. John never told you? No, I said. He said he was going to set up a meeting with John to talk about it. I said no. I told him he has to come out to a big meeting. No damage control.

The meeting is on Monday. I got 200 people to that meeting, plus the press. When John comes in I was working the crowd, leading cheers. "What do we want? We want to stay!" and "Hell no we won't go!". When the Mayor came everyone was booing him. The Mayor started to talk, then people started to tell him off. It was getting very rowdy. He said, "You people don't know what you want." John refused to talk to me. He didn't want to smell the air I was smelling. He was pissed off. Everyone was booing him. Total chaos.

No one liked me. But someone had to stand up for the people. We were fighting for something in our right. You just don't throw us out of our home. I choose to be here.

Weeks later on a plane ride to Washington, D.C. John sat down next to me. We decided we were a lot a like. Hard-headed, persistent. Neither one of us will ever give up. And he wants to get the job done, no matter what. That trip changed our relationship a little. I understood him a little better. He never thought that a resident, and a woman, actually stood up to him and bounced back!

Ramon Arroyo, Third District Town Committee, Hartford

When the issue of Charter Oak Terrace exploded in the newspaper, Carmen called me first thing, at 6 o'clock in the morning. "Have you read the paper?" No, I don't read the *Hartford Courant.* So I went and bought the paper and asked her what's happening. She didn't know anything about it, although John Wardlaw says she did know about it. We sat down and decided that we'd find out what was the real plan. We demanded that John Wardlaw tell us what he was going to do. We continued working together until she later aligned with John.

In Charter Oak, it's not that I was against the plan, but the process. You would be crazy to not want a better house. The Housing Authority never involved the community. I wrote letters to Mr. Cisneros [HUD Secretary], asked for Mr. Wardlaw's resignation. When the *Hartford Courant* came out with the news, we had a group of fifty people do a press conference asking him to resign. It was a total surprise to me.

Now you have an angry community that is being displaced. Nobody is saying anything. I'll keep banging the door until someone listens, here or in Washington.

I've been in Hartford seventeen years, and for fourteen of those years I've been involved with the community. I was in Jersey City, New Jersey, before that. In Hartford, I got involved with the Puerto Rican Political Action Committee, of which Eugenio Caro was the president.

Before the districts were redrawn, I did not spend time in Charter Oak. There was an unwritten rule that said you do not go into someone else's district. It wasn't our responsibility. If they don't ask us, we don't go in. Politically it doesn't look right. The change happened in 1991. When it came our turn to have it, we had a forum at the Charter Oak YMCA with [State Representative] Juan Figuero. We talked with the key players in the area. John Wardlaw was first. We found there was a lot of work to be done, as the area had been written off. We worked with police to get a community service officer there. We did so much, and were so upset when Wardlaw said he was going to raze the project.

When we first got involved, at the time that the new redistricting came in, we worked together. I thought he [Wardlaw] was sincere. For two years we worked on getting money for a sports complex, along with Senator Bill DiBella. Then this plan came out of the blue. I thought we had a working relationship, but I guess they were just patting my back so I didn't make any waves.

When people are involved, then they can demand. That's why I am in politics, to help people get involved. I'll keep doing it so long as I have the fire in my belly. Maybe that will be until the day I die.

I don't have any doubt that I'm respected in the political arena, maybe not liked, but respected. I want to make sure my community is also respected. We're not second class citizens. I'm a social worker by trade. Maybe the fire comes from my upbringing in a very caring family. There was always enough in the pot if someone unexpected came in. I'm not going to fix the world. But at least you try to do something that makes you feel good. I feel good trying to fix some of the injustices I see. Like the processes in Charter Oak.

"It's a ploy to rid the city of poor people and dilute the political strength of the emerging minority community," local politician Edwin Vargas said. [167]

Reading from a statement issued by members of the 3rd District Democratic Town Committee, Ramon Arroyo called Wardlaw Hartford 's 'biggest slumlord' and demanded his resignation and for a HUD investigation into his management practices. State Representative Ilia Castro also supported the call for his resignation, although later in the week she softened her position, saying she would be willing to listen to Wardlaw. [164]

At the February 27 meeting, a newspaper account described that Peters wandered through the crowd like a talk show host, and was sometimes jeered and heckled. But he vowed to work with the tenants to fine-tune a plan that he said would improve their lives.

"We are trying to create jobs and better housing," Peters explained. "Is that asking too much? . . . We have to work together." [164]

Mayor Mike Peters remembered this period:

> One mistake we made was that we didn't involve the whole community group in the planning. The story came out well before its time. Carmen went ballistic. She sat here in my office and gave me hell, and rightly so. She was most concerned about what would happen to the people who lived there. There was then a raucous meeting where we caught a lot of hell. But we learned from that, stepped back, made a committee and developed a good plan.
>
> I think Ramon [Arroyo] went knocking on doors telling people that we wanted every Hispanic to move out of the city. That wasn't the plan, and isn't the plan. We want to retain everyone who lives in public housing to remain in the city of Hartford. Ramon was getting people riled up. He was doing a disservice to his community. Anyone who tells me that they don't want a Charter Oak or Rice Heights to come down is out of their minds. To do that for a block of votes, you shouldn't be in politics.

John Wardlaw, Authority Director:

> I understand Ramon's position. I trust that he understands my position. I know that he is

dedicated, that he has the best at heart for the people. We don't get into difficulties over that. The difference is that I am non-political. He is very political. To remove that block of constituents represented a political situation. I didn't think that should be the driver of things that needed to be done.

I have a very strong conviction that is connected to a very strong personality. Ramon has a very strong conviction and a strong personality. If I could have done something differently to have stopped the misunderstanding with Ramon, I would have. Ramon for some reason just never got on board. If I had known what that was, I would have done that. We can accomplish a lot more as a team. That hasn't

Ilia Castro, Former State Representative

I have been in Hartford 27 years, and worked at the YWCA for seventeen years as the social service director. I came here to study in 1970. No family of mine was here in Hartford. I came here by accident. At the time there was an airline school here in the city. They recruited in Puerto Rico. Hartford was the closest city to New York, where I did have some family.

When I finished school, they didn't have a job in airlines. I found another job, stayed with some friends, and I've been here ever since. I was a pioneer for my family!

Why did I become a state representative? I didn't like politicking. Juan Figueroa was the state rep at the time for the Third District. He got a job in New York. He called me at home, asked me if I wanted to be the state rep, and I said, 'No, I don't want it. No way.' It was an honor that Juan thought I could do it. I thought about it, and two months later I decided to run.

I look back now on Charter Oak. I didn't like the way our Town Committee approached John Wardlaw. I didn't really agree with their [Housing Authority] first proposal. I always wanted it to be a project to empower the community to be part of this process. I think people were forced to leave Charter Oak with little explanation of their rights. The housing conditions were terrible. No one should have to live that way.

When I became state rep I sat down with Mr. Wardlaw. I wanted to form a committee to work on Charter Oak. He promised one thing, and then did what he wanted in the end. I think there was a lot of game playing. I really wanted to work with him. I think he has his own agenda. I pushed myself to be involved, to be at the table. We fought a lot. I wanted to make sure the community had a say in the process. There was always a lot of mystery there.

> been the case so far, but I anticipate and hope this is something that we can both put behind us.

The Changing Nature of Public Housing

The idea of tearing down large tracts of public housing represents potentially profound political and racial changes if public housing residents are dispersed across a city or region.

Some minority politicians 'have a vested interest in the maintenance of public housing, because they concentrate votes in wards that they control, and make safe seats,' said Douglas S. Massey, a professor of sociology at the University of Pennsylvania and author of *American Apartheid: Segregation and the Making of the Underclass.*

And given the history of urban renewal in America, in which city after city bulldozed poor minority neighborhoods and displaced people into public housing, Massey believes that poor Blacks and Hispanics are right to be wary of proposals to replace public housing.

"I think the key issue is what eventually happens to residents of current housing," Massey said. "They're pretty mistrustful of power structures in general, and of the white power structure in particular, and for good reason. I think there have to be political guarantees [when demolition takes place]." [168]

Greg Lickwola, Authority staff:

> Residents doubted that the Hartford Housing Authority was going to build anything back. There were big fights along the way, but we explained what we were hoping to do and that seemed to reassure people. There were a lot of false rumors out there about what we were supposedly doing or not doing.

Lillian Maldonado, Charter Oak resident, said that "When I first heard about the plans [for Charter Oak] I thought it was a joke. They'd talked about it for so many years I didn't think it would ever happen."

Chapter 17

Secretary of Housing and Urban Development Henry G. Cisneros 1995

By the time plans for ABC-side were announced in February 1995, demolitions were underway in Chicago, Denver, and Dallas, with more planned for complexes of 100 units or more throughout 1996 in Baltimore, Houston, New Orleans, Newark, New Jersey and Columbus, Ohio.

In many cases, according to a March 1995 *Hartford Courant* story, urban housing authorities were trying to replace high-rise towers or Army-style barracks projects, such as Charter Oak, with single family units — often housing that could be purchased by poor people — to try to create neighborhoods that would mix low- and middle-income people.

Federal housing policy is "no longer focused on what we give to people," said HUD's Joseph Shuldiner. "We're about building communities — and vibrant, healthy communities. A community should have an economic mix and a racial mix, too, of people." [168]

The momentum to remake Charter Oak was growing. The team involved Mayor Mike Peters, John Wardlaw, Hartford Housing Authority staff, HART leaders and staff, HUD's Joseph Shuldiner, Congresswoman Barbara Kennelly, and even Carmen Lozada, who had distanced herself from the Third District Town Committee's Ramon Arroyo.

Charter Oak's Carmen Lozada:

> They [Arroyo and the Third District Town Committee] did so many evil things to Mr. Wardlaw it was not funny. Even I could not believe what they did. They sent this letter to the Attorney General, laying out all kinds of bad stuff going on at the Housing Authority. I started to get scared to be with them. There's a lot of animosity between John [Wardlaw] and the Third District.

The final — and most important — player was about to join the campaign.

When Shuldiner was in Hartford in October 1994, he was asked to secure a meeting with the Hartford team and HUD Secretary Henry Cisneros. Shuldiner agreed to help.

HART leaders and staff worked several months with the Cisneros staff, as well as with staff from the office of Congresswoman Barbara Kennelly to nail down the crucial meeting for April 4, 1995. Also extremely helpful in securing an audience with the HUD Secretary was Othello Poulard of the Center for Community Change.

Lillian Maldonado, Charter Oak resident and participant in the April 4 Cisneros meeting

I moved to Charter Oak in 1989 from a shelter, where I had lived for five months. I was with my son who was one. I lived on Brookfield Street, on the corner near Dart Street.

I was happy when I moved to Charter Oak. It was so much better than the shelter. I had heard that it was better than Stowe Village and Bellevue Square. My sister, mother, aunt and cousin were living here when I moved in.

When the kids wanted to play I took them to the park. When I moved here I was scared. There were a lot of gang members. Once I came home and I'd left my door open. The kids had watched the door, stood beside it until I got home!

There was a shootout one day. I got home and my aunt and I were driving into the parking lot. We ran into the house, and wouldn't let my kids out of the house. A lot of drugs were being sold, on Admiral Street. There wasn't the freedom, and it wasn't where I wanted my kids to grow up. I couldn't afford to leave, even though I wanted to.

Cisneros became HUD Secretary in January 1993.

He started as an administrative assistant in San Antonio City Manager's office. In 1971 he was selected as a White House Fellow and worked as an assistant to Secretary of Health, Education and Welfare Elliot Richardson. In 1975 he was elected to the San Antonio City Council, serving until 1981.

In 1981 Cisneros became the first Hispanic mayor of a major U.S. city when he was elected Mayor of San

Jackie Fongemie, area resident at the April 4 Cisneros meeting

I moved to Connecticut in 1963 from a small town in Maine. I was only distantly familiar with Charter Oak. I didn't live there, it didn't pertain to me.

In 1984 and 1985 the Newfield Avenue bridge was out. Charter Oak residents came to some of the HART meetings at Batchelder School. They were concerned about emergency vehicles being able to get into Charter Oak with the bridge out. That was my first real involvement with the Terrace. In 1986 when I became President [of HART], I tried really hard to work with the Housing Authority. They came to meetings for a time, but for whatever reason they stopped coming. I was very much aware that there were a lot of problems there. Charter Oak was going downhill fast.

For several years I wasn't as involved in HART. Then in 1991 we had a meeting about policing at Batchelder School. Charter Oak came up somehow, and it really stuck in my mind. There was no reason for kids to be bitten by rats, to have to deal with gangs, shootings, drugs.

I felt we were ignored as a neighborhood because of Charter Oak and Rice Heights, from politicians to public safety to other services. Police used to call Charter Oak the 'DMZ'; they just wouldn't go in there unless they had to.

It was a crisis with the gangs. That's when we all really came together. No one should have to live like that. Gangs, school drop outs, no jobs. In a sense we could no longer ignore what was going on down the street from us, in our neighborhood. I remember talking with some of my neighbors about Charter Oak. Many said, if they choose to live like that, that is their problem. But how could we ignore that?

The politicians wanted to keep Charter Oak the way it was. They made the residents afraid. It was hogwash.

Antonio, the nation's 10th largest city. He served four terms until 1989. [186]

While in San Antonio, Cisneros learned to understand and appreciate the power of organized people, having gained experience at the hands of the institution-based organizing power, the Industrial Areas Foundation and its local leader, Ernesto Cortez. This early experience was critical to his recognition of the people-organizing effort in Charter Oak and his eventual support of the Hartford initiative.

The Cisneros meeting took place on April 4, 1995, at the Secretary's office in Washington, D.C. at 456 Seventh Street, on the tenth floor. The 18 participants included Mayor Mike Peters, Congresswoman Barbara Kennelly, Dennis King, (a top aide to Governor John G. Rowland), Jim Boucher and David Radcliffe of HART, resident leaders Jackie Fongemie, Jackie Velez, David Martinez, and Lillian Maldonado, John Wardlaw and Paul Capra of the Authority, HUD's Mary Lou Crane, and Joseph Shuldiner.

When Peters and Wardlaw were invited to the Cisneros meeting, reported the *Hartford Courant,* it put the two officials in a somewhat awkward position because a newly formed 'oversight committee' of Charter Oak residents and others had yet to decide on an official course of action for Charter Oak. [171]

At the meeting with Cisneros, the group talked about a concept for ABC-side, as well as future plans for Hartford's Stowe Village housing project. There was also a request to convert $19.8 million dedicated to D-side the previous fall to allow for demolition and new development. Finally, the group asked him to come to Hartford in September 1995 to personally tour Charter Oak. He said he would.

Cisneros gave the group an hour, and was impressed. "The collaborative with HART and the Hartford Housing Authority is exceptionally important and rare. We have a handful of cities with whom I have a special relationship: Atlanta, Chicago, New York, Miami, Philadelphia," he continued. "You are now among these. Raw neighborhood power, I think, is the solution to our urban woes. Your city has a real chance." [187]

Paul Capra, Housing Authority staff:

> We went to Washington in the early days of the Peters administration. Peters was rare in that he said public housing was a very important ingredient in the future of the City. We met at the Secretary's office. The Mayor led off the conversation by saying Hartford wanted to do things in a different way. Housing yes, but the Mayor talked about what we were doing at the time to revolutionize our school system. That triggered the Secretary, who gave a fifteen minute monologue on the importance of education.

Jackie Fongemie, area resident:

> It was pretty overwhelming to be in the meeting [with Cisneros]. It was the first time I'd been in a situation like that. Mr. Cisneros really listened, asked questions and seemed genuinely interested in what we had to say. He seemed really impressed with our neighborhood group. We had a lot of power in that room. It was very rewarding. I'll never forget it.

Peters said after the meeting that he was encouraged. He said Cisneros, a former mayor of San Antonio, Texas, spoke glowingly of Hartford and explained that he once jogged through the City's Bushnell Park during a visit.

"He said, 'Boy you really have a gem there,'" Peters said. "I told him, 'You give us the resources we need and we'll polish this gem real quick.'

"He felt that if we could come up with a very strong plan, things could happen. But there was no commitment made."

Dennis King, an assistant to Governor John G. Rowland, was also at the Cisneros meeting, and an important link to the State's involvement and support of Charter Oak and later Rice Heights:

> The administration became involved with Charter Oak when [HART organizer] David Radcliffe came to us in a very verbal way and made sure we understood what was taking place and what were the needs of that community. HART set up my first meeting with John

Wardlaw and several residents. I saw that he understood that 1940 housing wasn't working today. The administration has to thank HART for its involvement with Charter Oak and the Housing Authority. This was a bipartisan issue.

At our first meeting with Cisneros, of all the comments, those that were most moving and important came from residents. When he had a chance to speak to the residents, that made all of the difference. I remember Lillian [Maldonado] at the end of the table. You can see her eyes welling as she spoke about Charter Oak. She spoke from her heart. He responded back to her in Spanish, as she was having a difficult time with her English. For a moment it was as if they were the only two in the room. It was very powerful, a more important connection than any documentation or lobbying. At that very moment he was determined to make this happen. The sincere presentation by the team in Washington was crucial.

Mary Lou Crane, Regional HUD Director:

I think the key event was the meeting we had in Washington [April 4, 1995]. That was a very significant meeting. He [Cisneros] listened for an hour, saw the pictures. He spoke to me later and said I should stay very close to this situation. He could see there was a rapport in the group. He was very interested. He wanted to make a difference, and thought this might be it. A thousand units is a huge footprint in a neighborhood. The Secretary loved Mayor Mike, because as you know he too was a former mayor. He thought this would give our Mayor and the whole City a big win. It was a State with great political leadership. And it would help so many families. He really bought the argument that you shouldn't have to be a troubled housing authority to get funding. A very significant meeting, a landmark event in the turning around of Charter Oak. It was very wise of the whole group to come down and make the pitch. There was support across organizational units and political parties. A very impressive group to show him. Congresswoman Kennelly was involved quite a bit, and he had great respect for her. That was very important.

Clock Ticks as 'Committee of Forty' Meets

Back in Hartford, the future of Charter Oak was put in the hands of a forty-member committee charged with choosing among three proposals for the troubled housing project. The group consisted of area stakehold-

Dennis King, Assistant to Governor John Rowland

My family was from Lake Charles, Louisiana. I was born in 1953. The first ten years of my life revolved around questions of equality. I went to a separate school for example. The experience of the South never leaves you. My mother was on welfare, and raised three children on her own. I understood racism in its truest form. With what we see today with crime and urban decay, it's impossible for me to not be involved.

I worked with SNET [Southern New England Telephone] as a manager for a number of years. I had been involved in a number of civil rights issues since school trying to bring about some measure of equality. I interviewed with the Governor [John G. Rowland], expressed my views on issues. That's when I came on board. The Governor lived in Waterbury when I lived there. I lived in a housing project. We lived on separate sides of the track, but he understood that that side of the track existed. And as Congressman he spent quite a bit of time in those neighborhoods.

Housing is the answer, along with jobs. Poverty is one thing. You don't have the dollars to get out, but you're still striving. Being impoverished is another thing when you think you can't get out and don't even try. Ownership can began to instill the pride people need to get out of poverty. In public housing, we deny people the opportunity to achieve the American Dream. We subsidize so much we don't allow people to work. It's a form of slavery, without the whips and the chains. But the cycle continues, generation after generation, whether it's Charter Oak in Hartford, Father Panik in Bridgeport, or Berkeley Heights in Waterbury.

I remember the first time I was in Charter Oak. It brought back memories of my childhood. We lived in the same type of housing, and saw the same look in the eyes of the children, saw men standing on the corners — you could see the hopelessness and despair. We shouldn't have this in 1997. When will this cycle end? People can become too comfortable in that environment. Before the Governor was elected, we knew that housing revitalization was key.

ers, although only a handful were Charter Oak residents.

At the committee's first meeting in April 1995, Mayor Peters vowed to listen to tenants and not force upon them his desire to demolish ABC-side to make room for an economic development park. Peters said a quick decision was important, as HUD faced cuts that could sever funds to demolish projects.

"We have three or four months at the most to get a plan together," Peters told the group at the Mary Hooker School. "Whatever plan you come up with, we'll go back to Washington and sell it." [172]

On April 21, Shuldiner came back to Hartford to look at the north Hartford housing projects. He said HUD had two years of vision, and had better start producing. HUD had been more receptive to innovative plans in recent years as it found itself on trial with congressional budget-cutters. [188]

On April 27, 1995, Peters and Wardlaw told a packed neighborhood meeting at St. Lawrence O'Toole Church about Charter Oak plans. Peters said his goal was to create 750 jobs and at least 500 homes.

"Whatever we decide to do will be much better than it is now," Wardlaw said. "We have tried to provide every type of service to people in public housing. It doesn't work . . . people need jobs." [173]

By late April, it was still the desire of some to demolish all of ABC-side, but the plan agreed on by the oversight committee was a little of both: knock down 700, rebuild 200 units, and use the remaining space for business. At the time, only 653 of the 946 existing units in all of Charter Oak were occupied, with 293 unfit for human occupancy.

Many wondered what would happen to residents still in Charter Oak. There would be 363 newly rebuilt units of housing. Occupants of 200 units would get portable Section 8 certificates, allowing them to move into apartments of their choice, either in Hartford or outside the city. The Housing Authority would relocate another 200 subsidized units to privately owned buildings, providing landlords with what Wardlaw described as a guaranteed source of income. [175]

The Authority and Peters wanted to knock all of ABC down, but suggested that federal hurdles forced them to keep some housing there. (Dean Amadon, a local housing and planning specialist, suggests that the genesis of the notion to demolish all of ABC-side came from Stewart Murchie, then employed by Amadon's consulting firm and later an assistant to Mayor Mike Peters. Amadon remembers one Friday afternoon in the summer of 1993, Murchie was tossing around development ideas for different parts of the city. Having recently looked at the industrial space along the West Hartford/Hartford city border, Murchie thought it was a natural that the space on Charter Oak's ABC-side, then-occupied by some 600 units of housing, one day be dedicated towards total business use.) Some resident and political opposition also impacted on the decision to keep nearly 200 houses. And, Shuldiner said that HUD was in the housing business, so any plan had to have some housing. To push for total demolition at the time would have killed the plan.

"This is the first initiative undertaken in public housing in forty years," Peters said after the committee made its decision. "We want to make sure everybody is happy with the plan. What we're saying is: Let's make it work."

"We're going into the next century with some very good housing and some jobs," Peters said on May 3, 1995. "This is going to happen." [174]

Last Minute Opposition as Charter Oak ABC-side Funding Application is Sent to HUD

> "Charter Oak was temporary houses for people working at the gun factory. It was never intended to stay up so long . . . Go to the basement - it's mud. When it rains the water seeps through the cracks and we get horrible odors coming up from the basement . . . In April and May we have heat and you cannot shut it off . . . We can't live like that anymore. It's high time this place came down.
>
> "A lot of people always think of Charter Oak like we're the garbage. People remember the

> negatives but forget about all the good things that have come out of Charter Oak."
>
> — Carmen Lozada, quoted in July 31, 1995 Housing Authority application for ABC-side funding

As Wardlaw's staff pushed to meet a July 29, 1995 deadline for the ABC-side grant application, a flurry of last minute reactions came from Ramon Arroyo and Elizabeth Horton Sheff, the two remaining, or at least most vocal, opponents to razing Charter Oak.

A volley of letters were exchanged between Ramon and Wardlaw. The following is a sample:

> "It is clear to me from the news media reports that plans are being proposed and developed concerning the future of Charter Oak Terrace. It is also clear that those plans are being developed in forums deliberately calculated to exclude any meaningful participation by any and all members of the community who might disagree with Mr. Wardlaw's opinions on this matter. This is in direct violation of federal law, and Mr. Wardlaw and his accomplices need to be reminded of the legal implications of their actions."
>
> — Ramon Arroyo, July 25, 1995

> July 31, 1995:
> "For you to criticize this Agency's attempts in writing without even picking up the phone and inquiring as to your concerns verbally, is very unfair to the Housing Authority, and most important, to the people who are to benefit from our efforts."
>
> — John Wardlaw, Charles Groce (Chair, Board of Commissioners) [190]

More fire came from then Hartford City Councilperson Elizabeth Horton Sheff, at the time a candidate for Mayor in Hartford:

"He's [Wardlaw] a wordsmith — he can spin those words out there like a preacher," Horton Sheff said. "But what did he say? You know that Wendy's commercial? 'Where's the beef?'"

Wardlaw dismissed Horton Sheff's comments as the kind he encountered under former Mayor Carrie Saxon Perry. In those days, Wardlaw said, he was told by prominent city leaders to leave public housing alone; people like it and do not want to move out.

In a September 1995 Democratic primary campaign, Horton Sheff accused Mayor Mike Peters of running an 'apartheid' government that was trying to drive Puerto Ricans out of the City through 'ethnic cleansing'. [177] Local politician Edwin Vargas said the Charter Oak plan would disperse Puerto Ricans and "increase the white balance, the political clout of Mayor Mike's base" in the Southend.

These concerns weren't reflected by the larger voting population in the September primary election. Peters won handily with 80 percent of the vote.

Henry G. Cisneros Comes to Charter Oak

Following the April 4, 1995 meeting with Cisneros in Washington, HART and others worked through the summer of 1995 to secure Cisneros for a fall visit. Two weeks before Cisneros arrived in Hartford came some important news.

On September 1, 1995, Shuldiner wrote Wardlaw that the request to demolish, rather than rehabilitate, Charter Oak's D-side with money granted a year earlier had been approved. This approval allowed the conversion of the $19,754,250, Major Reconstruction of Obsolete Projects grant to knock down 266 units and rebuild 163. [192]

Two weeks later, on September 14, 1995, the nation's top housing official Henry Cisneros traveled through Hartford and promised to find another $21 million to finish rebuilding the ABC-side of Charter Oak.

Jackie Fongemie, area resident, remembers the September 14 Cisneros visit:

> Cisneros came to Hartford in September. We were outside. We took him on a bus tour of Charter Oak. We showed him Mary Hooker school, Prince Tech — we showed him what the neighborhood was about. We had a ceremony with him on D-side. Everyone was there. I was nervous and excited, but also comfortable. He made us feel so at ease, he was just a

HUD Secretary Henry G. Cisneros with Jackie Fongemie, community leader with Hartford Areas Rally Together. Event at D-side of Charter Oak, September 14, 1995.

> regular Joe. I get goose bumps thinking about it now. It was an honor standing next to him.
>
> You could tell the residents out in the audience were a little concerned. Here you have all these suits and ties sweeping down on their neighborhood. What does all this mean for us, people wondered. I don't know what that was like to live there, nor to go through all that change.
>
> Those gathered at Charter Oak's YMCA thanked Cisneros for the $19.8 million awarded to D-side, and asked him to use discretionary powers to get $21 million for ABC. He was also asked to come back to Charter Oak to announce the ABC funding once identified.

Standing amid Charter Oak's sagging, barracks-style units, Cisneros shared his fear that proposed congressional budget cuts could delay funding for a year or more. He had good reason to be concerned.

The Compromise Recision Bill had just been passed by Congress and signed by President Bill Clinton, rescinding $5.1 billion from HUD, including $700 million for priority replacement housing. [191] This was the pool of money that would have been available to fund the plans for ABC-side.

But Cisneros pledged to 'scratch' to find the funding, saying Charter Oak could serve as a national model for remaking public housing.

"We are going to find what we need to do the job," Cisneros said to a loud applause from 100 residents at the September 14 event. "It can be done in Hartford, and it can go across America."

Cisneros said Mayor Peters' victory in a primary the week before reaffirmed his support for the full Charter Oak plan.

"Anytime someone wins 80 percent of the vote, I'd say he's doing something right," Cisneros declared as Peters and other officials looked on. "The people are placing confidence in the City's leadership, and it's well-placed."

Mingling with the crowd, Cisneros asked HART's Jackie Fongemie why City Councilwoman Elizabeth Horton Sheff opposed the Charter Oak plans.

"Can I be honest with you?" answered Fongemie. "They want to keep the vote." [179]

With fewer residents in Charter Oak, there obviously wouldn't be the same number of votes. But were the leaving votes enough to make a difference in an election, in a neighborhood where voter turnout was traditionally weak?

Virginia Nunes, Third District Democratic Town Committee:

> Jackie Fongemie accused us of fighting [the Charter Oak plan] because of the votes. That is ridiculous. For one thing, Charter Oak has never been big on votes. The lowest turn out is there. People have given up. Most of our votes come from Behind the Rocks [neighborhood surrounding Charter Oak].

Ramon Arroyo:

> We fought because they were in our district, not because of votes. If we got 100 votes out of Charter Oak that would be a lot.

Mayor Mike Peters had a different opinion:

> I don't buy that Charter Oak wasn't important to elections. The first time I ran, there were 300

or 400 votes for me from Charter Oak. If you're running for state rep, it's a very big block of votes. It doesn't take much to swing 30 or 40 votes another way.

Cisneros Visits Charter Oak a Second Time

Cisneros wouldn't have come to town if not for Shuldiner and HART's involvement. The hallmark of HART is persistence. It has an agenda, it gets it done, and very few things stand in the way. Charter Oak wouldn't have happened without HART."

— Paul Capra, *Hartford Housing Authority, 1997*

On October 6, 1995, three weeks after the first Cisneros visit to Hartford, came the announcement of $21 million for Charter Oak's ABC-side. This remarkable figure represented more than 10 percent of HUD's total budget for projects of this type. Only 5 other cities in the country received money from this fund. Cisneros, as he had hinted on his first trip to Hartford, had used his discretionary powers to overcome Congressional cutbacks that had eliminated the kind of funding sought for the ABC-side plan.

"This is historic," said Mayor Mike Peters. "This will be a model for the rest of the country."

HUD's New England Director Mary Lou Crane said Hartford won out over scores of other cities because the Charter Oak plan represented a sweeping approach to improve housing while providing jobs and homeownership opportunities. She also cited wide support from tenants, community groups, City Hall, the State Capitol, and the region.

"It's good for the people, good for the community — it's going to upgrade the whole area," said Carmen Lozada of HUD's ABC-side commitment. "The people here no longer will have to live in filth and be embarrassed by where we live. We're going to be part of the community."

"We had everyone in the boat rowing the same way," Peters said. "That's how to get things done — teamwork. This is really, truly a great day for the city of Hartford." [180]

Mayor Mike Peters:

> When we went to meet with Henry Cisneros, (April 4, 1995) he liked the plans a lot. He liked the living and learning [formally called 'Campus of Learners'] piece of it, which was his idea. After that meeting he wrapped his arms around this project and said that this could be a model for the country. We worked with his office, the Housing Authority, the City of Hartford, HART — we kept working at it and before you know it we're granted $42 million. I'll take that every few months! I think it was a real good team. We all had the same goals. I knew it was going to happen because we had the right people in the right place at the right time.
>
> Henry saw a smaller city and a more immediate impact. $42 million doesn't go as far in a Detroit or New York City. I knew we were on the right track. Every meeting after that got better and better. When he came here the first time (September 14) you could see his enthusiasm for the city. A very large Hispanic community, which is dear to his heart. I think he saw the opportunities. He was here five times as Secretary. That's pretty outstanding. I've met with other cabinet members, but I've never met one like Henry as active and as involved.

At 10 a.m. on October 9, three days after the HUD announcement, Cisneros was back in Hartford for the second time in a month to personally deliver the final half of a $42 million package to transform Charter Oak.

The *Hartford Courant* recorded that Cisneros was greeted almost as a savior by some of the residents and dignitaries who filled the Charter Oak YMCA. They listened intently as he pledged to turn the project into a 21st century 'campus'.

"I think we have an opportunity to do something that is not being done anywhere in America," Cisneros told the crowd. "This is not about fixing windows and doors and roofs — it's about changing the very dynamics, the very concept of public housing in this country."

"It's important for HUD to support people who work so hard," Cisneros continued.

"You can do this — be the first in America. We will put in more money if the model works." [193]

Tenant Sheila Jackson reminded him of his whispered promise to her on his last trip that the City would get the remaining $21 million for its ambitious plans.

"After you told me that, I said a little prayer," Jackson said. "You are truly a man of your word. God bless you."

"In an era of tight purse strings, the river of coveted housing dollars flowing from Washington to Hartford had City leaders almost giddy with excitement," reported the *Hartford Courant.*

Mayor Peters earned a few laughs at the October 9 Cisneros event when, as the celebration was drawing to a close, he expressed to Cisneros his eagerness to get on with the project.

"Just give me the check, and I'll be a happy guy," Peters said. [181]

John Wardlaw, Authority Director

> I've seen quite a few Secretaries of HUD. I have not seen a Secretary that was more dedicated than Henry Cisneros. I don't believe that we will see a Secretary that was so in-tune with the plight of people living in public housing, and so in-tune with wanting to eliminate these incubators of social ills. He identified not with the property, but with the human piece. I have been in his company many times, and I have the utmost respect for him — not just for what he did in Hartford, but what he did in this country.
>
> I think those visits to Hartford by the Secretary were an opportunity to indicate his pleasure at what we were trying to do. By his being there he wanted the nation to know that something was going on here that was very important. He was the first HUD secretary to visit Hartford in my time here. Before, the Secretary would visit only if you were a big city or had a problem.

Mary Lou Crane, Regional HUD Director

I was always very impressed with John Wardlaw's relationship with public housing residents. That was very unusual for a director to know and care so much about the tenants.

Up to this day we [HUD] have the HOPE VI program for deteriorated, obsolete public housing. Big ticket program. John was always penalized because money was given out on degree of distress. Hartford just couldn't compete. Bad management got rewarded. Today you don't have to be a troubled housing authority to apply. So a Charter Oak is eligible for HOPE VI. Is it a wise investment of the federal dollar to go to some of these housing authorities? At the time these changes were being made, Secretary Cisneros was talking to Hartford and was saying we will have a special relationship with you and will get you some money. Hartford was the first city in the country to get this newly defined money.

The first time the Secretary saw D-side [September 14, 1995] it reinforced for him how important this was. He saw all those single family houses lined up across the street from D-side. His impression was what a contrast, between this very nice neighborhood of homeownership and then we've got these public housing barracks in a total dilapidated state. We need to make the public housing units look more like the rest of the area. This redoubled his resolve to make D-section happen. Then he saw ABC-side. He was overwhelmed quite frankly. He didn't realize how big a project it was, what bad shape it was in. He was somewhat discouraged. He was unhappy with what he saw. He thought the [Hartford] Housing Authority and residents could have done a better job at keeping the place up.

My interest in housing goes back to some volunteer work I did in housing as I was raising my kids — 4 in 4 years. I was active in the League of Women Voters in Cheshire, Connecticut, working on the Naugatuck Valley Regional Planning Commission. An opening came up on the planning and zoning committee. This was in the 1970's. I competed for the position and won. Waterbury was my hometown, and Cheshire was something of a bedroom community.

My first paying job was as Toby Moffet's district representative in New Britain. I moved from there to lobbying on behalf of community colleges, then heard about a job at HUD. I became special assistant for the area manager in 1979. I stayed at HUD in Hartford for six years.

Continued on next page

Maty Lou Crane, Continued from previous page

Then I became a community development rep, with UDAG [Urban Development Action Grant], frustrating at the time under the Reagan administration. They were doing nothing for housing. It was very hard for me.

West Hartford Housing Authority was looking for a director. They wanted to create public housing for families. I thought it was a great idea. I started there in 1990. We got $1.9 million from HUD to buy seventeen three family houses. I met John Wardlaw at the time through some work they were doing to help Hartford families buy in the suburbs.

Meanwhile people didn't like the idea of buying 17 houses in West Hartford. We ran into a stone wall. People started lobbying the town council to make us stop. And then death threats started coming in. "If you bring black people into West Hartford I'll blow you away." We had public hearings with 250 angry people. The City Manager said they were going to give me police protection. I thought he was joking at first. In the end we did it, but it was one of the hardest things in my life.

While I was doing this President Clinton got elected. I was having lunch with a politically connected friend of mine, who said we needed to figure out how to help Clinton get things done. I joked, 'well why don't I become the regional HUD director.' He thought it was a good idea! We mounted a campaign. [Connecticut Senator] Chris Dodd led the fight. Senator George Mitchell from Maine was Senate leader at the time. He had the idea that New England would figure out which jobs they wanted for which people. So they had this meeting. When it came to Connecticut, Senators Dodd and Lieberman said, 'well, we want HUD. We think housing is really important to Connecticut, and we have the perfect person for the job."

So I went to Washington in July 1993 for an interview with Secretary Cisneros. It went very well. A couple of weeks later I got a call from Senator Dodd who said, "It's done. I just talked to Henry. You got the job. Just don't forget Connecticut!" I was the New England Director of HUD. I oversee all HUD activity in six New England states. There are nine others like me in the country.

In the last three and a half years I've been all over New England, from Presque Isle, Maine to Burlington, Vermont. I spend most of my time in Massachusetts and Connecticut. I'm the first woman to hold the job. I paid the penalty. It was a real test of wills when I first got here. All the staff were male, and weren't happy to report to me. But I wasn't going anywhere.

Sheila Jackson, Charter Oak resident and one of the leaders that welcomed Cisneros to Charter Oak

I moved to Charter Oak in 1989. When I moved here it wasn't as bad as it became soon after. The gangs came, and it got a little crazy over there on D-side, especially at night with the guns and the cars zipping up and down the driveways.

I got a job not long after I got here, first at a hotel then up at Avery Heights Convalescent Home. We had nothing. It was scary. We had one mattress that the shelter gave us. They gave us some curtains which we tacked up to the wall until we got curtain rods. Housing didn't give us an icebox for three days until after we got there. It was cool enough that we could keep the baby's milk outside on the window. If my father had seen us he'd have been flipping in his grave!

It was nice, not wild, when I first came to the D-side. Not too many people hung out, and those that did stayed over by the Candy House, on the corner of Victory and Admiral Street. In the Candy House was candy, beer, some dope too. You could get anything you want. She's still in business today, right behind the Housing [Authority] office! They [Hartford Housing Authority] know half the stuff that went on out here. They didn't care.

Things changed in 1991 or 1992. Gangs started coming in more. Everybody wanted to be somebody. Little boys were bigger, and the way to be somebody was to be in a gang. Didn't have to go out of Charter Oak to be in a gang.

They never bothered me. Those boys only bothered those who bothered them. If anything they always had my back! A lot of that killing and stuff didn't come out of Charter Oak. Other gangs would sometimes come in — when they were havin' a beef with another gang and they thought they the other gang was gonna have a drive-by, they'd let you know. If you were outside, or your kid was outside, they'd bring your kid to your door. "Sister Sheila, you better keep them in the house. Somethin' is gonna go down."

This one guy Jo Jo would come over now and again. He's doing life after life after life now. Not baby life, but grandpa life. For killings. He liked to do stick-ups, and sneak attacks. Those he murdered never knew what hit them. He cried and cried. You could see his hurt. He just wanted to be somebody, to be accepted.

Somehow drugs get into these poor neighborhoods and they just kill the people. Package stores aren't in white folk's neighborhoods. But they're on every corner in black neighborhoods. The only time you see police down here is when you see too many white folks coming down here coppin'. Then they want to have raids, then they come down on our folks. Dealers know that white folks bring heat. "Beep me if you want drugs, I'll meet you somewhere," they'd say.

Charter Oak D-side.
Summer 1995.

Young people. Charter Oak ABC-side. Summer 1995

Chapter 18

Charter Oak Relocation and Demolition
1996

"Charter Oak was a symbol of urban decay. A confluence of negative, destructive tendencies. What's happened over the years hasn't helped, like putting cosmetics on a corpse. It had to come down. It had outlived its usefulness. I think the main motivation for the plans are to get rid of a blemish, not necessarily to help people achieve a better way of life. I think it is really important to focus on the people who live there, to help them become active in shaping their own lives. We need to improve the human condition, not just the conditions of the buildings."

— Art Feltman, State Representative, 1997

Now the real work began.
Hartford Courant, March 27, 1996

> Walking through the D-side of Charter Oak, Delores Jackson looked around and saw a ghost town. There were no squealing tires, no teenagers hanging out, no mothers walking children to school. Just rows and rows of empty, barracks style buildings boarded up with plywood. And silence.
>
> In five months nearly 500 people moved out of D- side. The rapid progress was a result of a snowball effect. As residents in the first phase began to pour out, residents not scheduled to go until the second phase followed their lead, taking the initiative to line up new places to live.
>
> Only 18 percent of D-side residents moved out of the City, most preferring to stay close to family, churches, and other familiar surroundings.

Juan Colon, Hartford Housing Authority staff

Juan Colon was the lead staff person for Charter Oak relocation efforts.

I came to Hartford from Puerto Rico in 1967. My family (six children all together) left because of high unemployment and better schools here. My parents thought that in time Puerto Rico would become a state, so they believed that their children should be able to communicate in both languages.

Whenever you face the unknown you are reluctant. Not knowing the language, the people. We had heard that Puerto Ricans weren't treated well here in the States, so we had to be ready. I've never felt discrimination directly myself. My mother was a teacher and my father worked in the Colt factory.

I studied health education, and coordinated a migrant program for those coming from Puerto Rico. There was a commission from the House of Puerto Rico after visiting the tobacco camps and the conditions there. In 1974, I argued about the need for more help on the mainland, and they asked if I wanted to help make the changes. So I helped handle contracts between the growers and workers and other things at a time when 7,000 came yearly to the Tobacco Valley [in Connecticut].

After working as the economic development coordinator of Miami for two years, under the hot sun, I got tired of that and came back to Connecticut in 1984 where I knew many people. In May of 1988 I came to the Hartford Housing Authority as housing coordinator. I started in Rice Heights and have since worked in most Hartford developments.

Now I am in charge of the relocation department, which we created when the idea of demolishing units started in 1994. Relocation had to be done safely and according to law.

The only way to eradicate the damage and bad memories in Charter Oak is by leveling and rebuilding the whole complex. Get rid of the cancer once and for all.

When the project started here, we had few problems. There was some concern about families moving out of Charter Oak and into other neighborhoods. On D-side when we started emptying the development, many people had said they wanted to stay, but quickly changed their minds. They must have feared the unknown, and also realized that there were better opportunities elsewhere. Many people also don't believe something will happen. So much money has been put into Charter Oak, millions of dollars — new roofs, windows. Unfortunately the structures were too far deteriorated.

> Many residents opted for rental-subsidy vouchers, financed by the federal government. Vouchers enabled poor families to move into private housing in Hartford and the region. [200]

Relocating wasn't easy for some Charter Oak residents.

Lena Roy:

> I made a good home in Charter Oak, even though the surroundings weren't very good. It took a big part of me when I had to move. Where I am now [in a home in South West Hartford] still doesn't feel like home. Here I don't have to worry about shootings, or drive-bys. My kids were upset and mad when we came here. They missed their friends and had to go to a new school. At first they didn't go outside. But now they play with dolls, play basketball and baseball, and even visit friends in Charter Oak. It's been a big adjustment.

Terrell Milner:

> I live on Kelsey Street now, but we'll be moving somewhere in the South End, near Kennelly School. Too small here now. Maybe in a few years I can get a house. The neighbors are so nice here, and it doesn't matter, color. The biggest adjustment is the quietness. It's so quiet here! In Charter Oak there was noise all the time. I like it, but it drives my kids crazy!

Mercedes Soto, staff for a youth leadership program:

> I came in the summer of 1995, on D-side on the corner of Admiral and Victory Street. I liked the feel of the community. The parents would visit often, and were very supportive of the counselors. In October 1995 we got word that families would be moving. By December half the families were gone. It was a very interesting time. I think those who moved out first were those who were most capable and worked hard to look for work or an apartment. A lot of them have continued to want their kids to be in the program.
>
> Some have moved back to Puerto Rico, and you can tell how strong the bonds were. Several call back and talk with their counselors.

> The relocation had different effects on different kids. For some it was a smooth transition. They were excited, had seen their new apartment. But for others you could see them struggling. They might find out the day before they move. They'd come by the office and say I'm moving tomorrow Mercedes. I said really? When did you find out? Yesterday. Are you packed? No. Where are you moving? I don't know. There's a lot of unanswered questions. Many were sad about leaving their friends. I worried about that, because transitions are hard for anyone of any age.

Sentiments from some Charter Oak young people on the changes in their neighborhood:

Felicia, twelve-year-old, Cotswold Street resident:

> I used to play tag, soccer, baseball, kickball, frozen tag. Played inside the fields in the backyards. Went to Batchelder School.
>
> I remember a little of the trouble in Charter Oak. It was sad. My mom told me that when I was little I used to be scared and cried when the shooting started. One day I was sitting in my room watching T.V. and I said, 'Mom, someone just got shot'. The ambulance went past. There were a lot of beatings. I used to be outside in my front yard helping my mom hang up clothes. There was this fight, and guys were beating up someone with sticks and poles. It was terrible. I was shocked.
>
> I'm gonna miss my friends when Charter Oak is gone.

Denise, twelve-year-old Caleb Street resident:

> It's fun in Charter Oak, except for the gangs. The gangs used to shoot a lot. I didn't like that. I would go inside and stay.
>
> I was raised in Charter Oak. I have two little brothers. My mom didn't want me to be outside after dark. I liked to hang around with my friends. But mostly everybody has moved now, some to East Hartford, some to Florida.
>
> We're moving too. I don't feel like moving. My mom wants to move. It looks all dead now.

Demolition of first unit on D-side, Victory Street. April 22, 1996.

Carmen, eighteen-year-old resident:

I've lived in Charter Oak for thirteen years, on Caleb Street. I like it. The people are close around there. Most of the time it's been alright.

My father is a hard working man. The people we used to live next to used to make a lot of noise. My dad used to go back and forth with them. I liked to play outside, but my dad wouldn't let me. I was frustrated, because my friends used to be outside. I understand now. I would do the same thing.

There were two gangs that were constantly fighting. They used to come to our side and fight. One time on Cotswold Street there were people throwing bricks and bottles at people on the other side of the street. It was crazy. I was upstairs in my room, watching.

This is the only place I know. I'm tired of it. I know that there is more out there somewhere.

Charter Oak is not like people make it seem. It's not a hell hole like some people out of Hartford think. There's violence no matter where you go. All my friends live in the South End, in houses. They couldn't believe I lived in Charter Oak. That was frustrating to me. I used to

Charter Oak D-side, along Chandler Street prior to demolition. Spring 1996.

Charter Oak D-side, along Chandler Street after demolition. Spring 1996.

Keith Henderson, area resident

I had grown up on Arlington Street since the fifth grade. Went to school at Batchelder, and had lots of friends in Charter Oak. I like Hartford. The shops, close to work, and I have access to fast food, without which I'd probably starve to death!

I didn't go into Charter Oak much as a kid, but I had a friend I would visit now and again. I went to his house and to his room. He was a big model car builder, and we'd play there.

I first moved to Dart Street [across the street from the D-side of Charter Oak] in 1978. I remember when the person who sold me the house was telling me that they were going to tear down Charter Oak Terrace and build a medical center. I knew it wasn't true, but he must have figured he couldn't sell the house! He said he shouldn't even sell now, because of all the doctors that would soon be moving in!

When I first moved here some of my friends and family thought I was crazy for buying that house. I had no credit then, just coming out of college. And I love the City, knew the area. I knew what I was getting into. There was the bad part, but I loved living there! There was a real feel of community.

Some summers were quiet, other years were nothing but trouble. Gun shots every night, and some days they'd set up speakers like an outdoor concert. All day long the same music over and over again, boom boom boom! Trying to sleep would drive you nuts. The police weren't too responsive then. In all the time I lived there, I never had trouble. Of course some gun shots, and back when the gangs were active you'd see them out and know something was up, standing at different corners and signaling to cars that went by.

I once saw a guy chase another down Dart Street with a semi-automatic weapon, shooting rounds off as he goes. From what I saw he didn't get hit. This was in the middle of the day! It was amazing. You'd hear shots all the time. It's the kind of thing you'd never have to think about in the suburbs. It was worst during the height of the gang violence. Guns every night, like a war zone. Despite that I never felt threatened. No stray bullets ever went through my home. They kept it to themselves. You just had to be aware what was going on, and be ready to move fast.

Over the years it was frustrating to see how much money poured into fix Charter Oak. You could have rebuilt the whole City! New roofs, then those would be destroyed, new windows and doors, then those would be destroyed. No accountability. Fix it, wreck it, fix it, wreck it. I hate to see that amount of money wasted.

To go from all of that noise and traffic to have it leveled. I was amazed when it was torn down. I'd never thought I'd see the day. Now it's like a park, and you can see Prince Tech!

I give a lot of credit to the Housing Authority, Wardlaw, and to HART. Without our pushing I don't think this ever would have come about. I hope the plans come about as they've been talked about. I think they will, because we'll be watching them!

> want my friends to sleep over, but my friends' moms wouldn't let them because I lived in Charter Oak.

April 22, 1996: Demolition Day

"Whoever built Charter Oak Terrace, they would be surprised to see their buildings still standing."

— Juan Colon, Hartford Housing Authority, 1997

At 1 p.m. on Monday, April 22, 1996, the jagged steel jaws of an excavator closed around the corner of a building on D-side's Victory Street. Tenant Carmen Lozada and several officials took turns running the giant John Deere machine. [197]

On that day, HUD's Mary Lou Crane said Mayor Peters broke a trend, where urban mayors distance themselves from housing authorities. [198]

There was a peculiar feeling in the air on the day of demolition, a mixture of excitement, happiness and sadness. Imagine seeing your house taken down? One writer said that many public housing tenants who live in buildings slated for demolition do not simply see buildings being torn down — they see a community being erased. [242]

Some thoughts from a few who were at the demolition:

Bill Gervais, Hartford Police Detective :

> I had mixed feelings on the day of demolition. That was their home, good or bad. I think people accepted the plans more as time went on. People saw it as an opportunity. That is one of the top ten most stressful things in one's life, to be moved or dislocated.
>
> There was nothing on D-side for the 300 families there. A community building was boarded up, but inside was a basketball court and a stage. Outside was a court, but it was covered with glass. It had broken rims, cracked pavement.

Richie Montañez, Principal at Mary Hooker Elementary School:

> I had mixed feelings at the demolition. On the one hand it signified the beginning of hope for the community. That made me happy. But it ended a whole generation of wonderful memo-

ries that many people had. It was the dismantling of the community. I had a heavy heart that day.

Carmen Lozada, Charter Oak tenant:

I felt like crying at the demolition. Before they emptied it I went for a walk. I could see the people hanging out the window in the summer, having their barbecues in the lawns. I had this terrible empty feeling like I lost my family. A part of us died. Then I thought, okay, some of these houses have many bad memories. We just had to do this, make the place more open.

Ramon Arroyo, local political leader:

I chose not to go to the demolition. I did not agree with what they were doing. I think there were a lot of ills in the area, but there were other remedies. I work on a daily basis in Charter Oak and there were a lot of good people there.

Mayor Mike Peters:

I felt very special about that day. But also some sadness. There's a lot of history in Charter Oak Terrace. I knew families who grew up there. I had friends there. But for the most part I was really happy. Let me tell you, we're not stopping with Charter Oak Terrace.

Juan Colon, Hartford Housing Authority:

On the day of demolition I felt sad in a way. Mostly every Puerto Rican that is in Hartford is connected one way or the other with Charter Oak Terrace. Most of us have had friends or family who have lived here.

Lillian Maldonado, Charter Oak resident:

I started crying when they knocked down my house. "This is my building!" I couldn't believe it! Now here on A-side [Maldonado moved there from D-side], it's terrible. Everyone moving into this side, many are selling drugs. I want to move, but this year is going to be too hot.

Jackie Fongemie, area resident:

The demolition was exciting, but there were too many people in business suits. There were so many people there! It was televised. It was fun to see Carmen [Lozada] operating the crane. There was a good feeling in the air. It brought people out to talk about what it meant to live there. There was also a sadness, like at a burial. I felt it was a time to put Marcelina Delgado and all the others who died to rest. Very sad.

Terrell Milner, Charter Oak resident:

I was happy when it got knocked down. I felt good because it was an opportunity for me. It was like knocking it down let me go on to better things. I think my mom misses it some. She was there for so long!

John Wardlaw, Authority Director:

The day of demolition was probably the highlight of all my years here. The bigger highlight though is to see housing being built over there.

Sheila Jackson, Charter Oak resident:

I couldn't believe it when they tore my house down. I went back three times after. It was over! I thought about all the good and bad times there. I'm looking forward to the new houses being built there.

Carmen Barone, Charter Oak resident:

I felt sad when the demolition began. I watched them knock down my house, even though I had a lot of bad memories there. It was like a cemetery at times, so much death.

Greg Lickwola, Hartford Housing Authority:

I was very excited to see the buildings come down last year. It's a beautiful piece of property, a real opportunity now to rebuild the community. I can't wait to see what it would look like a year from now! It takes a lot of patience, time and cooperation to make things happen. It's frustrating at times. You can't rush people out of their housing. Without all of the help we've had — from HUD, Congress, Mayor, HART — this never would have happened.

In Father Panik [Bridgeport, Connecticut housing project] it took them years to resolve problems. We haven't had any of those problems here.

Dennis King, Governor's staff:

On the day of demolition, climbing up into the crane reminded me of my senior year in high

Mayor Mike Peters, U.S. Congresswoman Barbara Kennelly at the dedication of the first new house on Charter Oak's D-side. October 1996.

> school at my last football game. Then I started welling up inside, and I tried to maintain my composure. I thought about where I started from. I had been labeled as having a learning deficiency. And I had severe asthma and was told I couldn't play sports. But I overcame all that, graduated with honors. Tearing down that unit was a great feeling. A great feeling.

Five months after the first building was taken down, there was not a unit left standing on D-side.

Then, for the first time in 50 years a new home was built in Charter Oak. It was on Dart Street near the corner of Chandler Street, constructed by Carabetta Construction.

On October 4, 1996 there was an open house to tour the model unit, one of 130 to be built in Charter Oak's former D-side. After the speeches, federal housing officials, representatives of HART, and dozens of tenants toured the model house, which was furnished with tables, chairs and couches donated by Luis Furniture from Hartford's Park Street. [202]

At the October 4 open house, Governor John Rowland's staffer Dennis King said, "When we met with Secretary Cisneros eight months ago, who would know that we'd be here today?" [204]

Rice Heights from the air. November 1997.

Chapter 19

Rice Heights
1997

"Years ago, what struck me about Rice Heights was the variation within the project. Some buildings are very clean and neat, with a welcome mat, pictures — some claimed the hallways as their space. Other units were the opposite. Really trashed, not cared-for. I got the sense people had different standards on how they wanted to live."

— Art Feltman, State Representative, 1997

I love Rice Heights! I'll die here!

— Ella Mae Sutton, Rice Heights resident

As 1995 rolled on, it became clear that Charter Oak was going to get some significant resources. It was logical to do something with Rice Heights, the state-funded sister to Charter Oak in equally poor condition. To remake Charter Oak without doing the same to the 388-unit Rice Heights, many felt, would be a waste of money.

Charter Oak is federally funded, Rice Heights state-funded. The Hartford Housing Authority is the landlord of both, managing the people and property. When it came time to push for Rice Heights, the Mayor and Hartford Housing Authority approached state leadership, made easier from the involvement of Dennis King of the Governor's staff in the earlier Charter Oak effort. Over the months since the meeting with Cisneros in Washington, King communicated much of the excitement and planning in Charter Oak to Governor John Rowland.

As early as November 12, 1995, a month after the second visit to Hartford by HUD Secretary Henry

Peter N. Ellef
Commissioner

State of Connecticut
Department of Economic
and Community Development
865 Brook Street
Rocky Hill, CT 06067-3405

December 18, 1995

Mr. John Wardlaw, Executive Director
Hartford Housing Authority
475 Flatbush Avenue
Hartford, CT 06106

Dear Mr. Wardlaw:

It is exciting to hear of the Housing Authority's plans for the redesign and construction of Rice Heights and Charter Oak Terrace. I believe that this project presents the City of Hartford with a unique opportunity to plan and implement a revitalization program which will positively effect every aspect of the lives of neighborhoods residents -- meaningful employment, adequate housing, education, recreation, etc.

You described, at our November 1st meeting, the Authority's vision for the recreation of the Charter Oak Terrace neighborhood. This initiative is founded on the Authority's successful application and award of Federal HUD funds for the redevelopment of the Terrace. You further described the Authority's desire to develop a comprehensive plan for the revitalization of the entire area, including Charter Oak Terrace, Rice Heights, New Park Road Commercial/Industrial Area, and the Zion neighborhood. I also believe that for any revitalization project to be successful, again the measurement is the positive impact on the residents' lives, a comprehensive plan is necessary to identify all of the issues, resources and opportunities.

The Authority and the State have an opportunity to develop a partnership to plan the future of this neighborhood. This agency fully supports this comprehensive approach to project development, and intends to commit funding resources, subject to availability of funds, and technical assistance, once the Authority has identified its needs.

As we see this plan, it has a minimum of four components, including assessments, in the following areas; 1) strategic revitalization goals, 2) physical development, 3)social and economic development, 4) implementation. I understand the you have formed a "vision group" to assess the project area and formulate development strategies, and have invited DECD to participate in this process. This Agency would like to emphasize that Charter Oak Terrace, Rice Heights and the adjacent neighborhoods should be planned as <u>one</u> project. The masterplan should state the project goals, identify and link all project activities, and develop the appropriate phasing plans. Finally, the City of Hartford should formally approach the Town of West Hartford to cultivate a partnership in this project.

We understand that the demolition of Charter Oak Terrace will begin during the first quarter of 1996, therefore, we feel that it is imperative that the Masterplan development begin as soon as possible so that the Charter Oak Terrace can be fully reconstructed as a City resource as determined by this Masterplan. Likewise, until recently, the Authority was engaged in planning activities for the future of the Rice Heights as a state funded moderate rental housing project. This planning should be subordinated to the Masterplan initiative, and the appropriate resources committed to this greater project.

Again, we are excited and willing to participate in this project. We are willing to meet as soon as possible to discuss the project scope and develop this proposal. Please don't hesitate to contact me or Chester Camarata, the project manager at 258-4229.

Sincerely,

Peter N. Ellef
Commissioner

PNE/pss
cc: Chester Camarata, Director, Infrastructure and Real Estate Div.
Michael Duffy, Director, Assets Management Div.

Letter to Housing Authority from Commissioner Peter N. Ellef regarding Rice Heights. December 18, 1995.

Cisneros, Mayor Peters said he had a verbal commitment from Governor Rowland to help redo the state-funded Rice Heights project. [183] This was an important and remarkable time, given that Peters and Rowland were in different political parties and then clashing on other City-State issues. The non-partisan nature to this point was critical, Cisneros had said, to his support of Charter Oak.

On November 29, 1996, the Authority submitted a request for funding to the State's Department of Economic Development (DECD), based largely on a $150,000 DECD-funded plan. The proposal called for a three-phase demolition of Rice Heights and the rebuilding of eighty duplex and single family homes at an estimated cost of $18,544,117. At the time, just 60 percent of Rice Heights was occupied. [211]

Jackie Maldonado, Rice Heights resident

I moved to Rice Heights in 1992. Before that I was on the D-side of Charter Oak with my mother and family. That was a real community. Then people started moving out. It became crowded with vandalism and drugs. I was looking for my own apartment, and because I was working I qualified for it.

When I moved in it was already deteriorating, but there were residents everywhere. Now there are only five left on my street [Pulaski Drive].

This is my little corner. I don't want to move. If you go up the hill, you find drug dealers, even more so now that people are moving out. They are very aggressive, and ask to sell you anything you want. They feel that is their home. It's disturbing to people that they can't let their children out to play. Yes it's less crowded, but more crowded with drug dealers.

It's not fit for living now [in Rice Heights]. Buildings are worn down.

I want to be involved every step of the way of the new development. I think our involvement so far has made a big difference. Things are getting done, we're being heard. Those of us most involved feel the power, and have more hope than in the beginning. More and more residents are getting up and speaking, where before people were afraid to say anything. Our tenant meetings are now where people go to get things done. On their own, people felt that they weren't being listened to.

Peter N. Ellef, Chief of Staff for Governor John Rowland

I was born in Athens, Greece and immigrated with my mother to the United States when I was three years old. We lived in a number of places, ending up in Old Greenwich, Connecticut I was raised by my grandmother who spoke very little English. My mom had three jobs, so she was always working. When we needed help, we called on our friends in the neighborhood. So we were really raised by our community. All of that had a tremendous impact on my life.

The only other constant I had as a child was the Boy's Club. My grandmother just couldn't take care of us full time in the summer. There was no day care in those days. So for three or four years my mother would put us on the train and send us to the Boy's Club in Greenwich. Those were the male models of my life. I played baseball and things that every kid wants to do while growing up. That's why I want to give back to the Boy's Club today. Later, I came back to work in Hartford and became involved with the Boy's Club here. That's how I met Bernie Sullivan [in 1998, Chief of Staff for State Speaker of the House Tom Ritter], for whom the Boy's Club was also very important.

I went to college right after high school. The only reason I was able to do that was because my mother was remarried when I was a junior in high school. The game plan up to that point was that I would get out of high school and start my own business, landscaping. My mother and I had saved for that up to that point. But my stepfather had some money, so all of a sudden I could go to college. I hadn't made any applications to college. I wanted to go to military school. It was in my blood. My father's stepfather was chief of staff for the Greek army, and an uncle who was an under-attorney general. I went to the Citadel.

While there I took ROTC, and from there went to the Air Force where I was a pilot — I flew bombers. Spent a year in Vietnam. After five years or so I decided to leave. I had three kids, and didn't see much of my family.

After, my brother got me an interview with Connecticut General Insurance company in Bloomfield, Connecticut. Worked there for 22 years, in sales and later management. I really enjoyed that, and moved on as managed care was coming on.

In 1995, a friend of mine came and asked if I'd like to work in state government. I thought it was a joke at first.

Contineud on next page

There had been additional evidence of the State's early commitment to fund a new Rice Heights. In a December 18, 1995 letter from Peter N. Ellef (then Commissioner of DECD) to Wardlaw, he writes that "it is exciting to hear of the Housing Authority's plans for the redesign and construction of Rice Heights and Charter Oak. The Authority and the State have an opportunity to develop a partnership to plan the future of this neighborhood."

"This Agency would like to emphasize," continued Ellef, "that Charter Oak Terrace, Rice Heights and the adjacent neighborhoods should be planned as one project."

Peter Ellef, Continued from previous page

Most people who know me in the private sector couldn't imagine me in the public sector. After several conversations, including some with Governor Rowland, I figured I was as well qualified as anybody to help with the merger of the two state agencies, housing and economic development. I had done a lot of similar work with Connecticut General, consolidating offices.

After we consolidated housing and economic development, it was clear we had to do more than just build things. We had to look at work, play, education, safety. Up to that point the projects were just brick and mortar.

These projects take a long time. Of all the projects we're involved with across the state, the one place where it all comes together, is Rice Heights. Or what we used to call Rice Heights. Rice Heights is a warehouse. No opportunities. I didn't understand it at the start, but I know now that there is a lot of community spirit there. But that spirit was never going to be accommodated.

I'm ashamed that we have allowed Rice Heights to exist. I'm offended by the conditions down there. Part of what the Governor wants to do is more with home ownership, in a serious way. But the programs out there won't do anything for most of those living in Rice Heights.

When my family came to America, we were dirt poor. It was a tough as it could get for us. I was part of my mother's struggle to make a better life for us. Rice Heights reminds me of that struggle. There's a part of me that will be happy when demolition finally takes place. As long as Rice Heights is standing, it reminds me of where I came from.

But mysteriously, State support for Rice Heights soon crumbled, threatening the full potential of the Charter Oak redevelopment.

Trouble in Rice Heights

On January 14, 1997, Linda Smith, President of the Rice Heights Tenants Association said, "There's so many things wrong with the place, probably it needs to come down. I'd like to see all the people who've stuck it out this long accommodated." [205]

The Authority sent the final funding application for Rice Heights to DECD on January 10, 1997. It called for building eighty duplexes and single-family homes on site. As late as early February, the Authority's Paul Capra had a good feeling about the funding, as the meetings on Rice Heights had more and more important people around the table. Mayor Peters was so confident of funding that he thought the money was literally sitting in the bank! DECD's Peter Ellef continued to talk publicly about how important the Rice Heights initiative was to Hartford and Connecticut. [212]

On February 21, two days after a tour of Rice Heights with State Representative and Housing Committee Chair Patrick Flaherty, a curious meeting was held in Ellef's office. Participants included Third District political boss Ramon Arroyo, State Representative Minnie Gonzalez and Flaherty. It was widely believed that the plug was pulled on the Rice Heights plan at this meeting.

Paul Capra said he and Wardlaw were summoned to the meeting in Ellef's office and were not told who would be there or what was on the agenda. Upon arrival, they found Arroyo and his protégé, new State Representative Minnie Gonzales, who reiterated their long-standing concerns about Charter Oak.

Capra said he and Wardlaw were asked to leave the room while the group and Representative Patrick Flaherty 'caucused' on the fate of Rice Heights.

A few days later, the Authority was notified by DECD that funding for Rice Heights was 'off the table' for reasons unknown at the time.

The Authority responded quickly with a letter to Ellef:

> "Instead of a dialog regarding the plans, Mr. Wardlaw found himself being questioned as to the Hartford Housing Authority's intentions. He found this even more confusing because Rep. Flaherty and Gonzalez had been provided with much of the same information prior to the meeting. In fact, Rep. Flaherty toured Rice Heights and the wider neighborhood and met with Authority staff and neighborhood leaders on February 19, just two days before. . ."
>
> "It is regrettable that DECD has seen fit after almost a year of heavy involvement, to withdraw from the planning process especially as it relates to Rice Heights, the conditions of which have reached a critical stage. . ." [214]

Ellef was troubled by constant changes in the Charter Oak plan, a reduction in home-ownership opportunities, the viability of a planned industrial park, and the $18 million price tag to raze Rice Heights.

The Authority was indeed several months behind on work in Charter Oak. According to Authority staff, the hope was that Rice Heights development would take place at the same time as Charter Oak, relieving relocation pressures. Despite evidence to the contrary, the State maintained that it was foolish to assume that Rice Heights was ever linked in anyway to the Charter Oak efforts.

On March 13, a source said that Ellef was still willing to cooperate. The problem was with Wardlaw, who he felt had dropped the ball. There was also some suggestion that the Mayor had not followed through on biweekly meetings to line up the details.

Peter N. Ellef, Chief of Staff for Governor John Rowland:

> Rice Heights was taken off the table, but before the Ramon [Arroyo] meeting. In fact, the meeting with Ramon was part of the process to put it back on the table. I took it off the table, because the Hartford Housing Authority wanted to take $18 million and build another Rice Heights. No homeownership. No community input. No talk of educational component. We

Ella Mae Sutton, Rice Heights resident

I started doing some domestic work when I was 11, earning a few dollars a day. Ended up doing that kind of work for 40 years. This helped me provide for my mother. I worked for Mandell on the corner of Albany and Vine after school. She would give me fifty cents to bring home, and she'd keep the rest, teaching me how to save. She was a big influence on my life, teaching me values. She told me that what I was doing was an honest days work, and that I had nothing to be ashamed of. She said once I learned this that I would never be hungry, never be out of a job. She wanted me to be good at it. She taught me well. That experience taught me that I could make it.

I lived on Vine Street. I had my first child when I was 13 and 1/2. I had had a son who'd gotten in very bad trouble as a child. I raised seven children. My husband walked away from me while I was carrying my fifth child. He ended up in prison. Turns out my husband wasn't taking care of business, and one day all of my belongings were all on the curb. I got a one room apartment. I was on assistance and got $80 a month. We lived on that, the 6 of us.

And my son was in prison for murder. They gave him twenty to life. I was all worn out holdin' on. I never gave up, but I ended up having a nervous breakdown. Too much, too long, the doctors said. But still God had been good to me.

My counselor said I needed to start over. She, Mrs. James, was the love of my life! She helped me get into Rice Heights in about 1975. I lived at 113 Coleman, at the corner of Flatbush Avenue, on the second floor. Eventually I went back to work. You had to be married and working to get in. I wasn't married anymore, but got in because of my medical condition.

It was very nice when I first came out here. My oldest daughter was already living here. I loved it out here. I was working at the time, but I'd go to the center for meetings. For kids there were winter and summer programs. Linda Smith (Rice Heights resident) made so much of this happen. She had a lunch program.

I got to know many people out here. The kids called me Granny. Now many are grown up, and when they leave they come to say goodbye. I see them born here, grow up here, leave here. Some did very well.

I wasn't boastin' or hollerin' too loud, but I let people — I call them my children — know that I worked, that I went to church. I hope that some of them listen. Everyone knows me, and they look out for me, walking me home from church or helping carry bags up to my apartment. They all know that I'll walk with them if they need help.

I love Rice Heights! I'll die here.

> wanted to address all at the same time. It got worse when the newspaper polarized the issue, reporting the opposite of what was happening and saying the State didn't want to commit the $18 million. I also got a little extreme when we found the Feds wouldn't share some of their 'soft costs' — such as design plans — from Charter Oak. It's the penny the Feds attempt to control costs at the expense of the nickel that they spend controlling it. Regulations got in the way too. Damnedest thing I every saw in my life. No one was really being obstructionist. It wasn't worth stopping the project.

Over the last few days of February and into March, a number of high-ranking local and state officials (including Mayor Peters, State Senator John Fonfara, and State Speaker of the House Chief of Staff Bernie Sullivan) joined the fracas to figure out what happened, and what could be done to rescue the project

Then came an all-out explosion.

On March 13, 1997, a front page story in the *Hartford Courant* by Tom Puleo brought to light the Rice Heights troubles. What was known to a few up to that time was now known to all. The story:

> An ambitious plan to remake public housing has been jeopardized by the State's refusal to chip in a crucial $18 million the Mayor says was promised.
>
> The State's Economic Development Commissioner, Peter N. Ellef, has concluded that Hartford is drifting and hasn't clearly outlined its plans for Charter Oak, said his spokesman, Chris Cooper.
>
> So the State for now won't allocate $18 million needed to rebuild Rice Heights, a state-owned housing project next to Charter Oak.
>
> "We've had all kinds of discussions with the State as it relates to Charter Oak," said Wardlaw. "They have everything that we have. I don't know what brought this about."
>
> Some officials speculate that Gov. Rowland may be pulling back the money because Hartford already is slated to receive state aid to bail out its schools and complete other projects. Rowland's office denied that claim.

> The standstill presents the possibility of Hartford ending up with the brand new Charter Oak on one side of the street and the same old Rice Heights on the other.
>
> That prospect isn't sitting well with HART, which has a meeting tonight.
>
> "Rice Heights is a festering, oozing eyesore," said area resident and HART President Marilyn Rossetti. "We cannot leave Rice Heights as it is and possibly accomplish anything in Charter Oak. The state would be doing a huge disservice if it doesn't give us back that money."

John Fonfara, State Senator:

> I became more involved when there was a danger of this coming off the table. Ellef had some concerns with John Wardlaw's plans and where they were going. I had a lengthy conversation with Ellef, telling him how important Rice Heights was to us. He assured us that it would get moving. I trust him. Matter of fact it was at a HART meeting where I first represented that it would go forward.

"The commissioner wants to be part of the solution," Ellef spokesperson Chris Cooper said. "He thinks there is a plan that, at least, most people could get behind. The question is, 'What is that plan?' "

On the night that the *Hartford Courant* broke the Rice Heights story, there was a meeting organized by HART at the Broadview Community Church. Area resident Jackie Fongemie said "that the reason we're coming together is that the momentum has been lost. The interest and excitement from the State has dwindled. The community wants to know what is going on."

"The bottom line is that we thought the State was in for $18 million for Rice Heights," Mayor Peters said. "We're just going to go ahead with our piece. We're hoping the State will get back on board." [206]

Mayor Mike Peters sought to assure residents at the meeting that plans to rebuild public housing would not be jeopardized by the State's unexpected decision to withhold $18 million in funding. Peters said that he intended to resolve problems during an upcoming meeting with Peter Ellef.

Linda Smith, Rice Heights resident

I moved to Rice Heights October 15, 1974. I had five children all together, three boys, two girls. We had owned a house on Baltimore Street, and my husband got sick. We had to give the house up. We'd moved around and couldn't find a decent place with good rent. So we went over to Housing, and signed the papers. A week later we went to look at the apartment, and liked it, and moved in soon after.

It was beautiful when we first moved in [to Rice Heights]. Grass, no graffiti, no broken windows, no drugs. A family-type area with kids playing in the park and people cooking in the backyard. We had baseball games too. Just about everyone who lived here — who wasn't working that time of day — ended up down at the park. Park and Rec used to also bring a trailer in the summer. They'd have puppet shows, or show a movie. The only level place for them to park was on Brookfield near the maintenance office. The kids would sit up on the hill and look down at the show.

Ray Montiero was the president of the Tenant's Association at the time. My neighbors told me I should go to a meeting. I went to one and got really involved. We used to go marching for this, demonstrating for that — for things that we thought weren't fair. When I first moved in I paid $90. They wanted to raise the rent. So we marched, carried signs, gave speeches. I'm not a political person. I just wanted to help make the place I lived better.

Changes started when they let people who either weren't working or weren't married to come into the project. That was the early 1980's. It was families only at one point. Things got pretty bad, but I never wanted to move. I've always felt safe. Sometime I'd come back from church at night. Some of the kids would see me. Some were selling drugs. But they'd take my key, carry my bags, and make sure it was safe for me to go into my building. I feel like I belong here.

Most of the drug dealers here now don't live here in the project. Many of them don't even live on this side of town. It's like going to work for some of them.

One time I got a knock on my door at 5 a.m. They said someone had been hung in the park. We thought they were joking at first. I quick checked my kids, and they were all okay. My husband went to the park, and at the slide, sure enough, was a man hanged to death there. There was nothing for him to push off on, so we think he had some help. For a long time the kids wouldn't go down there to play. That's one of my worst memories living here.

It would be so nice for those who want to stay can stay. But most of us won't be able to afford to stay. It will be sad, but I'll make do.

What's the deal with Rice Heights?

OUR TOWNS

Hartford

An impasse between the state of Connecticut and the Hartford Housing Authority over the proposed renovation of Rice Heights has created a sense of apprehension among the more than 200 families living there. That's not fair or healthy.

Residents deserve to know what the state, the property's mortgage holder and the housing authority, which holds the deed to the land, plan to do. Earlier this year, the authority proposed demolishing the project and building single-family homes and duplexes to the tune of $18 million.

The state, however, will only commit $6 million, which the authority says would only cover the demolition costs. There are no funds for new construction, which has put the plan in limbo.

Rice Heights is located next door to Charter Oak Terrace, which is being demolished and rebuilt under a federally funded project. The housing authority sensibly wanted to adopt a similar model at Rice Heights. Charter Oak's revitalization effort with the U.S. Department of Housing and Urban Development has received national praise.

Peter Ellef, the state's economic development commissioner, is questioning the authority's plan to build 80 new structures at Rice Heights — 20 single-family homes for immediate purchase and 60 duplexes to rent with the option to buy. The state wants to see fewer rentals and more ownership.

But this sticking point and other concerns about details of the proposed development are premature. It doesn't make sense to argue over the features of a new affordable housing development if there isn't a serious commitment or the funding to move forward.

Meanwhile, tenants need to be kept informed of the project's status so that they can make some decisions on their own.

One of several Hartford Courant editorials on Rice Heights.Sept. 4, 1997.

"We thought there would be a big master plan put together with the State . . . and we're going to put it back on track," Peters said. "I'm not even worried about this." [207]

Following a meeting with Ellef, Mayor Peters said on April 4, 1997, that Ellef wanted to move ahead. The State had an idea that it could do the development for less money, and would put together a plan. [216]

"I want to make sure the community gets on board [in Rice Heights]," Mayor Peters said on May 22, 1997. "One of the mistakes we made [in Charter Oak] was that the community wasn't involved as much as they should have been." [208]

Tenants at Rice Heights felt their homes were being neglected and progress there was too slow. A Rice Heights group met steadily throughout 1997, including tenants Linda Smith, Ella Mae Sutton, Migdalia Burgos, Margarita Davila, Nickie Jones, and Jackie Maldonado. Staff support was provided by Tasha Coleman and Charmaine Craig of the neighborhood group HART.

Linda Smith said it was very difficult not knowing what was going to happen next.

"Everything's up in the air," Smith said. "It's very frustrating. We don't know what to do."

Rice Heights from Pulaski Drive. October 1997.

"Even though we're still on the table, I feel like I'm living in a dome," said Ella Mae Sutton, a twenty-year Rice Heights resident. "This is all very uncertain. The least they can do is let us know how much time we have before we have to get out. Let's treat us like human beings. We're not buildings." [220]

On October 1, 1997, after eight months of uncertainty, the State publicly agreed to demolish Rice Heights. A private developer would build 80 new homes.

Peter Ellef:

> "At the same time we redo Rice Heights we want to develop fifty acres in ABC-side of Charter Oak. Bernie [Sullivan, Chief of Staff to Speaker of the House Tom Ritter] and I have an employer lined up, a company that has been out of the City but wants to come back in.
>
> "The first building or two will be built by the State, and we will work with the technical school and the State Labor Department to create a training program. You'll be able to walk to work. It will employ eighty people.
>
> "My mother had this expression, all you need to do is earn $100 clear a week and own a $30,000 house. She raised three kids alone, and made rent for 30 years. I think if you can make rent you should be able to own something." [222]

"It looks like things are really moving along," said Rice Heights resident Jackie Maldonado. [223]

Peter N. Ellef, Chief of Staff for Governor John Rowland

Along the way we met a developer who ran Jimmy Carter's Habitat for Humanity. We asked them, why couldn't we in a public way do what you did for Habitat? They said the biggest problem in the north east was the expense of the land. In the case of Rice Heights, we own the land, so it's easier to do some creative thing to allow those living there now to come back. I want to help people own there.

Since the beginning we haven't wanted to dictate what will happen in Rice Heights. I want people in Rice Heights to tell us what they want. Here's one example. Beyond housing, I wanted to have a new recreation community center. Right across the street from Rice Heights is now a Boy's and Girl's Club. Jackie Maldonado [Rice Heights resident] said to me, why do I want to send my kids to the Club, and I go to the recreation center across the street? She was right. Now we'll build them together in an expanded Boy's Club so the parents and the children can be together.

I want this to happen. I'll know what it looks like when it is complete: the Vo-tech school training piece is in place, employer is up and running, houses going up.

Without Charter Oak, I think Hartford would have, in time, asked us to do something serious with Rice Heights. We're normally asked to do little things, like defer interest on the principal. What does that do for people?

We're moving due north on this project, no matter what other people want to do or what other bureaucratic bullshit comes up. We've got to keep this on a short timetable — this building season. Longer than that, the project will be dead. I am not going to be deterred. Neither will Bernie Sullivan or Jackie Maldonado, and others who have a passion for this.

In October 1997, Peter Ellef was promoted to Governor John Rowland's Chief of Staff.

Chapter 20

A New Beginning
1997 to the Present

"This neighborhood had been ignored for so long. The focus was only on the bad. It was finally a dream come true. I believe in my heart that this will become the best neighborhood in Hartford."

— Jackie Fongemie, area resident

In 1941, public officials and residents could hardly contain their excitement at the Charter Oak they had built, a project expected to last some sixty years. The buildings stood for the projected six decades, but the community within collapsed years ago. Why? Poor design and construction from the start, changes in federal housing policy, historically weak local management of the housing stock, a regionally stagnant job market, and changing family structures all contributed to the devastation that became Charter Oak Terrace, Rice Heights, and public housing in many of the country's inner cities.

Given the life, death and rebirth of Charter Oak and Rice Heights, it is clear how *not* to create healthy and vibrant public housing. It is also evident that some issues contributing to the environment in today's public housing are beyond the control of local, state, or even federal governments. For example, it is clear that local economies are impacted by global business decisions that can draw jobs from the city, leaving behind those families with the least ability to move. But as the 1990's come to a close, and with the Charter Oak story as evidence, a great deal can be done at all levels of government and across organizational units to create

Construction of a new unit along Dart Street in Charter Oak's D-side. Winter 1997.

the public housing communities that residents, taxpayers, and voters deserve.

The Charter Oak and Rice Heights story, says the Authority's Paul Capra, came about as a "confluence of history."

> And the stars all crossed two or three years ago, with a cooperative mayor, state and federal officials, HART — all up and down the line. That along with the "one-for-one" and the flexibility of large money — that happened altogether.
>
> (The 'one-for-one replacement' rule was in place until 1996, and said that for every unit of public housing taken down, a new one had to be built somewhere else.)

Arthur Anderson, President of Imagineers housing program in Hartford:

> We couldn't have done Charter Oak 15 years ago. The rental market was too tight. There would be no place for the people to move. And the suburbs didn't want these folks.
>
> This took a confluence of events to occur. Nobody can say 'I made this happen to Charter Oak'. John Wardlaw, the Mayor, the Tenant's Association, HART, HUD — each one had a

New construction along Dart Street in Charter Oak's D-side. Winter 1997.

> veto to stop it, but none could have made the changes alone.

Federal regulation changes, the right people at the right time, and the funding all lined up to make it happen. And many believe that none of these events would have mattered had not people's attention been drawn to Charter Oak by gang violence.

Bill Gervais, Hartford Police Detective:

> When the shooting really got going and started spreading throughout the city, the next thing you know everyone is involved and wants to help in Charter Oak. It wasn't like that in the beginning. Eventually the buildings would have had to have been shut down the way they were deteriorating. But I think it took that crisis to get to where we are now, with the demolition and all.

Charter Oak and Rice Heights Today

In 1941, 1,000 families lived in Charter Oak Terrace, and nearly 400 in Rice Heights. In mid-1998, just 200 total remained in both projects. Although relocation has gone relatively smoothly, the Connecticut Civil Liber-

Charter Oak Tenant Association President Carmen Lozada and worker operate crane to remove first ABC-side building. February 19, 1998.

ties Union has brought a lawsuit against the Housing Authority, suggesting that some residents were forced to leave, or to take an apartment in an area no better than the one they left. The impact of this case is unclear, but it is not expected to affect the construction in the former Charter Oak.

The D-side is all gone now, and in its place 130 units will be rebuilt by the end of 1998 as single family and duplex homes. A unique feature of the new D-side is that all homes are wired to allow for computer hookup and interface with area educational institutions. This 'Campus of Learners' feature has become a national model for new public housing.

More than 200 Charter Oak residents have signed up for homeownership classes, and with creative financing, many will be able to purchase their first home.

Demolition in ABC-side began in February 1998. The Housing Authority decided in late 1997 that no houses would be rebuilt on the site, allowing all 55 acres of ABC to be used for business. There is hope that a commercial tenant, already identified, will occupy a

A new home along Dart Street on former D-side of Charter Oak. February 1998.

portion of the site by the end of 1998, with jobs for up to 80 public housing residents.

In Rice Heights, evolving plans call for relocation to continue through the summer of 1998, followed by the demolition of all 388 units. Eighty new homes will be built by DeGeorge Home Alliance of Cheshire, Connecticut.

(Since the State of Connecticut verbally committed $6 million for the relocation of families and demolition of Rice Heights in October 1997, there have been several fights in the eight months following that could have jeopardized the revitalization of the project. As late as May 1998, there was a very real chance that Rice Heights would not go forward. The largest remaining stumbling block, close to resolution at the time of publication, involved the transfer of the Rice Heights land from the Hartford Housing Authority to the State. Several sources reported that the Authority, as part of their formal transfer of Rice Heights to the State, has requested that the State's Department of Community and Economic Development forgive several million dollars in debt incurred at two other Hartford housing projects.)

U.S. Senator Chris Dodd and Authority Director John D. Wardlaw watch as the first building is taken down on Cotswold Street in Charter Oak's ABC-side. February 19, 1998. Dodd said, "I'm looking around here, and I don't see Charter Oak Terrace. I feel like I've crossed into Hartford's suburbs."

John Wardlaw has a dream, said one staffer, of fixing or rebuilding all public housing in Hartford by the year 2000. He talked about the implications of the local work in public housing:

> I think we'll be on the road to possibly change America. Not just public housing, but cities. One reason Hartford isn't working is because we have too many people in Hartford who aren't working. Public housing was built for the working poor. Now, we have no income people who can barely meet their minimum needs. The idea was you save money on your rent, and use the rest to improve yourself. The whole purpose of public housing changed.

A New Hartford?

This local renaissance has not been limited to just the projects. Hartford's labor and real estate markets have recently shown signs of new life. There is also a marked improvement of confidence in the City, with several neighborhood and downtown initiatives of historic proportions in the works.

In other Hartford neighborhoods, the City of Hartford is embarking on the demolition of several hundred unsalvageable residential buildings, an effort on a scale not seen since the slum clearance projects of the 1940s. And less than a mile from Charter Oak and Rice Heights, Trinity College has begun a $100 million project to rebuild the southern one-third of the Frog Hollow neighborhood. In a few years this area will boast several educational and medical research facilities.

Dozens of other improvement efforts are underway in parks, schools, secondary business strips and downtown Hartford. The more serious among these plans and activities include a Hartford convention center, several new hotel buildings, a revamped Civic Center, and a major road redesign effort to allow for greater pedestrian access from downtown to the Connecticut River.

When this work is done, much of Hartford's physical environment will have been remade, resulting in a less densly populated city with more mixed-income residential areas. Few cities in the country are undergoing the transformation now taking place in Hartford.

Nearly sixty years have passed since Charter Oak was built. How will those with a stake in Hartford sixty years from now view the results of today's work? Time will tell if future leaders will appreciate today's efforts to apply the lessons of the past, and to boldly remake public housing and cities into the new millennium.

Afterword and Appreciation

How This Story Was Created

"A lot of people always think of Charter Oak like we're the garbage. People remember the negatives but forget about all the good things that have come out of Charter Oak."

— Carmen Lozada
Charter Oak resident

This book has been an idea for several years. Beginning in March 1997, I began actively researching, sorting materials and conducting recorded interviews. I thank Charmaine Craig and Cindy Reaves for their help in collecting the stories of several Rice Heights residents. We are grateful to those who shared their insightful and often touching experiences on life in Charter Oak and Rice Heights.

Time and again I was overwhelmed by the power of these stories. Many have made significant contributions to their families and communities. Even as the units crumbled, there continued to live remarkable people with an uncommon strength and will to survive. John Wardlaw:

> You can travel anywhere in the country and find a product of public housing. Right here in Hartford. You can go to any bank, insurance companies, the state capitol — everywhere there are people who came from public housing.

The story of Charter Oak and Rice Heights would not be complete if it details only the changes in structures. To fully understand the history and lessons of Charter Oak and Rice Heights, the unique, important

Photographer Tony DeBonee as a young resident of Charter Oak Terrace.

stories of those who lived there must also be remembered.

This book has only scratched the surface of those stories. For every one person mentioned, many hundreds are not. Dennis King:

> I think there are many who will never have the opportunity to comment on what Charter Oak meant to them. I'm lucky to have that chance now. There have been so many who have struggled before I came on the scene, and there will be many more long after I'm gone to make sure that that the struggle continues.

The narrative has been improved immeasurably by the pens and encouragement of Dean Amadon, Jim Boucher, David Beckwith, Linda Bayer, Paul Capra, Lynne Lumsden, Mike Smith, Chauce Perreault, and Greg Robertson.

I am also grateful to those who read and challenged early drafts of the book, including Ted Carroll, Tasha Coleman, Justin Foley, Jackie Fongemie, Dennis King, Greg Lickwola, Carmen Lozada, Liz Pond, Marilyn Rossetti, Mercedes Soto, and John Wardlaw.

Without the financial support of Mass Mutual, the *Hartford Courant*, the Hartford Housing Authority, and the Connecticut Light and Power Company, this book would not have been possible.

Hartford's Tony DeBonee, a former Charter Oak resident, shared several great photos. Mercedes Soto also loaned several photos. Most early pictures are from Hartford Housing Authority archives. Those taken after 1991 are by the author. Liz Noli created the attractive book cover. The steady, thorough reporting of *The Hartford Courant's* Tom Puleo and Lisa Chedekel added a great deal to our understanding of more recent events in the life of Charter Oak and Rice Heights. Finally, I am indebted to Jon Harden and the staff of Southside Media for their interest in publishing this project.

The recorded interviews of 50 area residents and public officials and all supporting materials are available for public study at the HART office (227 Lawrence Street, Hartford, 860-525-3449) or the Hartford Collection at the Hartford Public Library (860-543-8641).

It has been my honor to help record this remarkable story.

David Radcliffe
Hartford, Connecticut
June 1998

About the Author

Born in Ohio, David Radcliffe spent his youth in Brockway, a small town in the hills of western Pennsylvania. He has worked in and around Charter Oak Terrace for the last seven years as a community organizer with Hartford Areas Rally Together (HART). Radcliffe is also the author of *The People's History: The Story of HART,* published in 1995.

End Notes

HT = Hartford Times
HC = Hartford Courant
HHA = Hartford Housing Authority
1. Slum clearance, 12/20/1934, HT
2. Housing body appointed, 5/24/1938, HC
   Items from Charter Oak time capsule (October 1941):
3. Hartford National Bank check to tenants of Charter Oak
4. Commissioner note
5. Pamphlet on rental defense housing in Hartford
6. List of contractors
7. List of Hartford Housing Authority staff
8. Need for housing war defense workers
9. List of defense industries
10. Charter Oak tree fragment, 10/6/1941, HT
11. Charter Oak dedicated, 10/5/1941, HC
12. Ease tight rents, 10/18/1941, HT
13. Functional design, 10/18/1941, HT
14. Public housing, 1/11/1941, HF
15. Authority faced with other work, 2/23/1941, HC
16. Come from overcrowded houses, 4/18/1942, HC
17. Allen named Executive Director, 1941, ?
18. Move to better conditions, 10/18/1941, HT
19. Nelton, Bellevue ceremonies, 1941, HT
20. Salvage efforts, 1942
21. Kennelly — ration board, 4/7/1943, HT
22. Dimout, 11/19/1942, HT
23. Soldiers guard industry, 12/9/1941, HT
24. Airraid, 12/11/1941, HT
25. Lottery for Hartford draft, 2/10/1942, HT
26. Rations, 5/4/1942, HT
27. War bond rally, 9/8/1942, HT
28. Oak connected to low income, 4/1/1947, HC
29. Gas heat for Charter Oak, 2/18/1960, HT
30. Fifty years of vo-ed, 11/6/1960, HC
31. Prince Tech opens, 9/16/1960, HT
32. Parent protest, 5/8/1968, HC
33. HHA aide gets jail term, 11/25/1975, HC
34. Oak problems, 12/16/1975, HC
35. Rats, 9/10/1976, HC
36. $418,000 grant, 4/3/1977, HC
37. $1,000,000 grant, 9/30/1977, HC
38. Too large for one manager, 5/13/1978, HC
39. Oak proposal, 6/7/1978, HC
40. Deaths, 6/19/1978, HC
41. Grant $14 million, 8/11/1978, HC
42. Rep. Cotter tours Oak, 9/19/1978, HC
43. Oak plans compete for $10 million, 2/5/1979, HC
44. Dumping ground, 10/11/1978, Hartford Advocate
45. First Annual Report, HHA, June 1938

46. Second Annual report, HHA, 12/1/1941
47. Fourth annaul report, HHA, 5/4/1943
48. Fifth annual report, HHA, 1943
49. Sixth annual report, HHA, 1944
50. Seventh annual report, HHA, 1945
51. Eleventh annual report, HHA, 1949
52. Tobacco crops, 1955, HC
53. Local Puerto Ricans, 3/3/1954, HT
54. Puerto Ricans in Connecticut, 4/25/1954, HC
55. Too little, too many, 5/2/1954, HC
56. 3,000 Puerto Ricans, 4/24/1957, HT
57. Newest neighbors, 5/4/1957, HT
58. Newcomers to Hartford, 3/15/1959, HC
59. 2,000 Puerto Ricans arrive to farms, 3/13/1964, HC
60. Puerto Ricans trek to Hartford, 8/31/1969, HT
61. Island in the American mainstream, 1/1/1981, HC
62. Shrinking tobacco fields, 1/11/1981, HC
63. Young shoulders, 1/14/1981, HC
64. Political punch lacks power, 1/15/1981, HC
65. Mary Hooker obituary, 5/14/1939, HC
66. Project named Rice Heights, 9/7/1948, HT
67. Fred Rice obituary, 8/16/1953, HC
68. Rice Heights flood, 9/27/1955, HT
69. Report shows Rice Heights in poor shape, 9/28/1955, HT
70. Rice Heights ignored, 4/12/1974, HT
71. Grant to rehabilitate Rice Heights, 3/27/1978, HC
72. Minister camps out, 6/16/1979, HC
73. Advertising from HC front page story on Oak, 10/4/1941
74. Charter Oak model, 8/10/81, HC
75. History of Hartford Streets, by F. Perry Close, CT Historical Society, 1969
76. Mayor letterr to HHA re fence repair, 5/15/1959
77. 'Controlled integration' letter from City Manager, 3/1/1965
78. Families avoid high rent, 11/17/1965, HC
79. Jobs draw Puerto Ricans, 3/15/1970, HC
80. Return to island, 3/16/70, HC
81. Class room tragedy, 3/18/1970, HC
82. City is popular for Puerto Ricans, 7/16/1971, HC
83. State getting worse, 11/21/1976, HC
84. HHA 12th annual report, 1950
85. HHA 13th report, 1951
86. HHA 14th report, 1952
87. HHA 15th report, 1953
88. HHA 16th report, 1954
89. HHA 18th report, 1956
90. HHA 20th report, 1958
91. HHA 21st report, 1959
92. HHA 22nd report, 1960
92a. HHA 24th report, 1962
93. HHA 25th report, 1963
94. HHA 28th report, 1966
95. HHA 1972 annual report

96. HHA 1977 annual report
97. HHA 1978 annual report
98. HHA 1982 annual report
99. HHA 1985 annual report
100. HHA 1987 ten year overview
101. CT State housing study, 1947
102. Profile of Hartford housing, 1979
103. Hartford atlas (1855, 1880, 1896, 1909, 1917, 1920)
104. HHA 1991-1993 annual report
105. Rice Heights fact sheet, 10/1991
106. Charter Oak fact sheet, 10/1991
107. How to save money and improve public housing, Center for Community Change, 1994
108. Gang drive-by, 7/30/1992, HC
109. Solidos grow, 10/19/1992, HC
110. Nike death, 10/21/1992, HC
111. Hispanic involvement, 10/31/1992, HC
112. meeting agenda, HART, 9/3/1992
113. meeting notes, HART, 11/16/1992
114. "From My Perspective", by John D. Wardlaw, 12/1992
115. Boy's Club, 3/27/1993, HC
116. Gang mayhem, 6/9/1993, HC
117. Curb city gangs, 6/11/1993, HC
118. Fighting for respect, 8/29/1993, HC
119. City ask state troopers for help, 9/8/1993, HC
120. City curfew, 9/8/1993, HC
121. Curfew enforced, 9/10/1993, HC
122. Police high visibility, 9/11/1993, HC
123. Violence quelled, 9/20/1993, HC
124. Gang members targetted for arrest, 10/7/1993, HC
125. Lagging enrollments, 12/9/1993, HC
126. City teen hurt in shooting, 11/26/1993, HC
127. City acts to deter violence, 10/30/1993, HC
128. meeting agenda, National People's Action, April 1993
129. meeting notes, HART, 7/13/1993
130. Wardlaw urged to run for Mayor, 7/21/1993, HC
131. Meeting notes, HART, 9/15/1993, HC
132. HHA fact sheet, children in public housing, 11/1993
133. Martin Luther King day, 1/18/1994, HC
134. Marcelina shot in drive-by, 3/27/1994, HC
135. meeting after Marcelina's death, 3/31/1994, HC
136. Bentsen to visit Hartford project, 4/2/1994, HC
137. Bentsen vows to rid city of guns, 4/5/1994, HC
138. Whose streets are these?, 5/1/1994, HC
139. Gang member testifies in girl's death, 6/30/1994, HC
140. Charter Oak to get face-lift, 9/28/1994, HC
141. Rebuilding housing projects, 10/5/1994, HC
142. Plans would demolish Charter Oak, 10/19/1994, HC
143. A new Charter Oak, 10/24/1994, HC
144. Hartford battles blight, 12/10/1994, HC
145. Action could turn around housing woes, 12/11/1994, HC
146. Fifty years of Charter Oak, 12/18/1994, HC

147. Four dead, 12/31/1994, HC
148. Charter Oak march, 1/18/1994, HC
149. Teen attack, 1/26/1994, HC
150. Meeting notes, HART, 2/15/1994
151. Last days of Panik, 8/7/1994, HC
152. HHA leter to Mike Peters, 8/8/1994, HC
153. Why Iran Nazarro, by John Wardlaw, 8/19/1994
154. Charter Oak survey, HART, 8/1994
155. HHA plans for ABC Charter Oak, 10/13/1994
156. Joseph Shuldiner biography, 1994
157. Shuldiner itinerary, HART, 10/18/1994
158. Hispanics see themselves, 12/16/1992, HC
159. Hispanic exodus, 1/30/1994, HC
160. Move to mainland, 8/14/1994, HC
161. Puerto Rican rapid rise, 10/20/1994, HC
162. Hispanics seek fortunes, 3/18/1996, HC
163. Experts say zone could fly, 2/26/1995, HC
164. Tenant's jeer city plan, 2/28/1995, HC
165. Good ideas for Charter Oak, 3/1/1995, HC
166. Zone gets cautious support, 3/1/1995, HC
167. Party line, 3/4/1995, HC
168. Raising hopes, 3/19/1995, HC
169. Indict Solidos, 3/15/1995, HC
170. A year later, 3/26/1995, HC
171. Mayor, HUD talk, 4/5/1995, HC
172. Quick decision on Charter Oak plans, 4/6/1995, HC
173. Residents, officials discuss plans, 4/28/1995, HC
174. Revised Charter Oak plans, 5/4/1995, HC
175. Private housing part of plan, 7/15/1995, HC
176. Hope in public housing, 7/24/1995, HC
177. Peters calls victory mandate, 9/13/1995, HC
178. Guilty verdict, 9/15/1995, HC
179. Cisneros visits Hartford, 9/15/1995, HC
180. Housing plan wins funding, 10/7/1995, HC
181. Model for nation, 10/10/1995, HC
182. Housing plan praised, 11/9/1995, HC
183. Mayor Mike method, 11/12/1995, HC
184. Jackie Fongemie, 11/13/1995, HC
185. Ramon Arroyo letter, 4/12/1995, HC
186. Henry Cisneros biography, 9/1993
187. Meeting notes, HART, 4/4/1995
188. Meeting notes, HART, 4/21/1995
189. HHA Charter Oak plan, 7/31/1995
190. HHA letter to Ramon Arroyo, 7/31/1995
191. HHA letter, 8/25/1995
192. HUD letter to HHA, 9/1/1995
193. Meeting notes, HART, 10/9/1995
194. Mayor makes rounds, 1/25/1996, HC
195. Trigger man named, 2/2/1996, HC
196. Charter Oak dreams, 3/27/1996, HC
197. Beginning of the end, 4/23/1996, HC
198. Rebuilding by tearing down, 4/26/1996, HC

199. Testimony tells of crime, 5/3/1996, HC
200. Project gets going, tenants do too, 6/4/1996, HC
201. High hopes for a model house, 10/3/1996, HC
202. City has homes, and hope, 10/5/1996, HC
203. Officer a good scout to city youths, 10/30/1996, HC
204. Meeting notes, HART, 10/4/1996
205. City's housing plan revamped, 1/14/1997, HC
206. State decision may blight Hartford plans, 3/13/1997, HC
207. Peters optimistic on housing renewal, 3/14/1997
208. Input sought from Rice Heights residents, 5/23/1997, HC
209. Rice Heights dedication, 9/7/1948, HT
210. Peter Ellef letter to HHA, 12/18/1995
211. HHA plan to DECD, 11/29/1996
212. Meeting notes, HART, 1/23/1997
213. Meeting notes, HART, 2/24/1997
214. HHA to DECD letters, 3/1997
215. Meeting notes, HART, 3/13/1997
216. Meeting notes, HART, 3/21/1997
217. Meeting notes, HART, 5/21/1997
218. Meeting notes, HART, 5/1997
219. Hope seen for grant, 8/7/1997, HC
220. Limbo status of Rice Heights, 8/22/1997, HC
221. HHA letter to Peter Ellef, 9/11/1997
222. Meeting notes, HART, 9/18/1997
223. Plan back on track, 10/2/1997, HC
224. Meeting notes, HART, 11/6/1997
225. Time stands still, 10/4/1997, HC
227. "The Magician of Hartford", by Rob Gurwitt, Governing Magazine, July 1996
228. Landlord Training Program, Portland Police Department
229. Survey city buildings, 4/11/1941, HT
230. 2000 new families, 5/20/1942, HT
231. Negroes ignored in industry, 2/21/1941, HT
232. First Negro to Trinity College, 5/3/1948, HT
233. HHA explains Negro status, 5/17/1955, HT
234. Where can a Negro live?, Part I, 5/19/1956, HC
235. Where can a Negro live?, Part V, 8/23/1956, HC
236. "Aqui Me Quedo", by Ruth Glasser, 1997
237. Promise got lost in projects, 7/13/1987, HC
238. American On Line, FDR/New Deal, 1996
239. "Power Broker", by Robert A. Caro, Knopf, 1974
240. Do Housing Authorities have a future?, 12/1997, Governing Magazine
241. CT Secretary of State booklet: Sites, Seals, Symbols
242. "An Invisible Community", by Sudhir Alladi Venkatesh, The American Prospect, September/October 1997
243. "People's History: Story of HART", 1995
244. "Hartford Immigrants", Robert Owen Decker, 1987

Interviews (taped between April and December 1997 by David Radcliffe, Charmaine Craig and Cindy Reaves):

Charter Oak residents:
Carmen Lozada
Terrell Milner
Lena Roy
Sheila Jackson
Carmone Barone
Aida Maldonado
Jerry Martin
Laura Taylor
Dan Lynch
Fr. Bill McCarthy
Marilyn Romano
Ron Copes
Lenny Texidor
Pancho Taylor
Lillian Maldonado
Faith Barnes
Maria Ayala
David Santos
LEAP young people

Rice Heights residents:
Ingrid Johnson
Ginger Foster Manns
Lucinda Thomas
Jackie Maldonado
Linda Smith
Nicki Jones
Dana Reaves
John Fonfara
Ella Mae Sutton

Others interviewed:
John Wardlaw, director HHA, 1977 to present
Paul Capra, director of planning HHA, 1992 to present
Mary Lou Crane, regional HUD director, 1993 to present
Barbara Kennelly, U.S. Congressperson, Connecticut-1st District, Democrat
Mike Peters, Mayor of Hartford, 1992 to present
Greg Lickwola, director of development, HHA, 1992 to present
Richie Montañez, principal, Mary Hooker Elementary School, 1990s to present
Charlotte Chambers, teacher, Prince Tech School, 1960s to present
Art Feltman, State Representative, 1996 to present
Keith Henderson, area resident
Dennis King, Aide to Governor John Rowland, 1990s
Jackie Fongemie, area resident
Mercedes Soto, staff, LEAP youth program, 1990s
Ramon Arroyo, Chair, Third District Town Committee, Hartford, 1990s
Joe Croughwell, Chief of Hartford Police Department, 1993 to present
Bill Gervais, Hartford Police Department, 1970s to present
Juan Colon, HA staff, 1980s to present
Ilia Castro, State Representative, mid-1990s
Peter N. Ellef, former Director of State Dept of Econ Development, Aide to Governor Rowland, 1990s
Arthur Anderson, President, Imagineers. Hartford-based administrator of federal Section 8 program.

Other key people not interviewed:
Russel H. Allen, first HHA director, 1939
Berkeley Cox, second HHA Board Chair, 1941
Daniel Lyons, HHA director, 1953 to 1977
Henry G. Cisneros, former Secretary of Dept of Housing & Urban Development, 1990s
Joseph Shuldiner, former HUD director of Public and Indian Housing, 1990.